You are a
person of
consequence.

Be brave.

Visit **TheBraveHabit.com** for additional resources:

The Brave Habit workbook

The Brave Index assessment

The Brave Habit course

The Brave Habit speeches and workshops

Videos, podcast episodes, and more

Want to buy a lot of copies for your team or event? Please email orders@toddhenry.com. We can even create a custom edition of the book for your group.

PRAISE FOR *THE BRAVE HABIT*:

"Todd's book will change the world we live in and the lives of the people who read it. Grab a copy for the people you care about, and save one for yourself."

SETH GODIN, author of *The Song of Significance*

"Every leader looking to make an impact needs this guide by their side. *The Brave Habit* is a roadmap for meaningful change."

DORIE CLARK, author of *The Long Game*

"I have read thousands of inspirational books over the years, but what set *The Brave Habit* apart is the way it drove me to make clear, concrete, and practical changes in my own life. If you want to be brave and make bolder moves right now, start with this book."

TOM RATH , author of *StrengthsFinder 2.0* and *Life's Great Question*

"Choosing to step forward when you want to step back ... that's the moment that saves the world and unlocks your greatness. This book helps you to be brave."

MICHAEL BUNGAY STANIER, author of *The Coaching Habit*

THE
BRAVE
HABIT

TODD HENRY

MARION HOUSE

Published by Marion House

For rights inquiries:
Accidental Creative
7672 Montgomery Rd., #201
Cincinnati, OH 45236
support@accidentalcreative.com

The Brave Habit

ISBN 979-8-218-30341-9 (pbk.)
ISBN 979-8-218-30342-6 (ebook)

CONTENTS

Now is all you have.

ORIGINS

"You cannot swim for new horizons until you have courage to lose sight of the shore."

— WILLIAM FAULKNER

I almost died when I was fifteen years old. I was playing in a varsity basketball game when I suddenly felt a tightness in my back. The coach pulled me from the game and had me stretch on the sideline, but I couldn't shake the pain so I sat on the bench for the remainder.

Later, I awoke in the middle of the night unable to move my legs. I rolled out of my bed and crawled arm over arm into the hallway where I screamed for my parents to help. They called an ambulance and I was transported to a local hospital, where an initial X-ray revealed a mass the size of a grapefruit in my abdomen.

The immediate fear was cancer, but after emergency exploratory surgery they discovered that the mass was actually a swollen muscle. I had an infection so dangerous that the muscle had expanded to well beyond its normal size, pressing some major nerves against joints in my back and causing immobility and extreme pain.

Over the next few days, friends and family cycled through my hospital room. It seemed odd that they were choosing their words very carefully, but I didn't realize at the time that many of them probably thought those would be the last words they'd ever say to me. Tears in their eyes, they would encourage me and share fun memories of our times together. As I got worse, the local doctors were at a loss for what to do. So, they transferred me to the nearest hospital with an infectious disease unit, where I spent several weeks wasting away in a hospital bed as the doctors tried their best to save me. At one point, the lead doctor told my parents "*If* I can save him, I'm going to have to pump him so full of antibiotics that there will almost certainly be major side effects." Of course, my parents told him to do what was necessary.

The antibiotics worked. It was nearly a miracle. Thirty-five years later I've experienced no side effects other than the ability to turn invisible on demand. (That's normal, right?)

The infection waned and I began to regain the ability to move my legs. However, I was a ghostly shadow of my former self. I had entered the hospital at six-foot-three and one hundred eighty-five pounds, and I was leaving weighing in at one hundred thirty-five.

I had lost fifty pounds in just a few weeks. My muscles had atrophied from lack of use. I was the very definition of "skin and bones".

My doctors told me that I would likely be able to walk again, and probably be able to exercise, but that playing basketball was unlikely, especially given that I was about to enter my junior year of high school. This crushed me. Basketball was my true love at the time and the thought of not being able to play again felt like the end of the world.

The first part of my physical therapy regimen was to simply regain the ability to control my legs. Taking two steps would sometimes be a full hour's work. Over weeks, I regained my ability to walk with assistance, then on my own. I began to re-gain weight with the help of family friends who supplied me with endless protein shakes from their employer. By mid-summer, I was not only walking again, but was running. I began attacking the steps in the high school gym, sprinting up and down them to get back in shape. By the fall, I was shooting basketball, and by the time the season rolled around I was back in full form. By my senior year, I led our league in scoring and rebounds and was invited to play in our state's all-star game.

I tell this story not to relive the "glory days" of high school sports, but because my near death experience caused a fundamental shift in both my outlook on life and my behavior.

Before my illness, I was relatively shy and self-conscious, taking life as it came, and avoiding circumstances where I could fail. Afterward, I was transformed into a different person. I realized that any failure paled in comparison to what I'd experienced in the hospital. After being subjected to the indignity of hospital gowns, sponge baths, and playing the role of "human pin cushion" for a few months, I lost all of my self-consciousness. I began to publicly perform music I'd written. I asked girls who were - let's be honest, *way* out of my league - to go on dates. But most importantly, I gained the perspective that life can be vanishingly short and that nothing is promised to any of us except for this moment, here and now, in this place.

I experienced the urgency and imminence of the *now*.

Even though I would never wish anyone to go through what I experienced, for a teenager this shift in perspective was a massive gift. In fact, it has shaped much of my life in the years since.

I am writing this book with the hopes of giving you a sense of the same perspective I gained in the wake of my health crisis without the need for the near-death experience. I hope to help you attain a new appreciation for the urgency and imminence of the now. Because *now* is all you have.

THE COWARD

Inside of you lives a coward.

This coward is obsessed with self-preservation, self-protection, avoidance of risk, harm to reputation, failure, self-disappointment, and wishful thinking. The coward engages in frequent doubt, blame, regret, self-loathing, and catastrophizing.

But, also inside of you lives the capacity for *unspeakable* bravery.

Bravery is doing the right thing even in the face of fear, following intuition where it leads, acting where others shrink from opportunity, defending those who cannot defend themselves, boldly speaking your ideas into the world, and sacrificing what's necessary to bring them into existence.

No one aspires to cowardice, yet many still choose it every day. They fail to speak up because they're afraid of being wrong. They take the easier, more comfortable path instead of the one that could lead to immense return on their effort. They join the crowd instead of standing firm against the populist tide. They justify their cowardice as prudence.

And that's the funny thing about cowardice: it often comes disguised as wisdom. No one *chooses* to be a coward, or at least they don't call it that. They argue that they are doing the most practical thing.

"I can't share my idea in the meeting because it may not be ready for prime time yet, and I don't want to risk being laughed at. The wisest thing is to just wait."

"Someone else is probably more equipped than I am to take on that project, so the wisest thing is to just pass."

"Even though I disagree on principle, if I side with the popular opinion now, I can spend that political capital later to achieve my goals."

"I shouldn't have that difficult conversation with Jill because it's just going to lead to a miserable month at the office. The best thing is to hope the situation resolves itself."

Each rationale *seems* wise, but is it? Is it possible that these are simply excuses we make for our own cowardice?

There is nothing wrong with desiring comfort, but rarely is the comfortable path the most gratifying one. As poet Khalil Gibran wrote in *The Prophet*, "Verily the lust for comfort murders the passion of the soul, and then walks grinning in the funeral."

If you feed your cowardice, you slowly murder your own soul.

However, you have the choice to be brave. You can train yourself to act instead of deferring, to speak instead of holding your tongue, and to embrace discomfort instead of shunning it.

You can develop the *habit* of bravery. Through everyday practice, you can build a deep reserve of courage ready to deploy at a moment's notice. You can turn bravery from a difficult decision into an instinct.

That is the goal of this book. If you read each chapter and spend time with the exercises within, you will discover a new perspective on life, work, and relationships. You will learn things about yourself that you never knew, and re-discover elements of your productive passion that have fallen dormant for far too long.

You will awaken your *passion of the soul*.

Let's begin.

Bravery is a *discipline,* not an inevitable outcome.

CHAPTER ONE

BRAVERY IS ABOUT MOMENTS

"Life is a succession of moments, to live each one is to succeed."

— CORITA KENT

Your moment is coming. It will be a time of testing for you - of belief, character, will, strength, vision - and how you respond could prove an inflection point in your life, for better or worse.

However, your moment is probably not some major life change or big, public decision. Rather, it's likely to be a small, private test.

For example, your moment could be a difficult conversation that needs to happen even though it's very uncomfortable. Or, it may be the chance to give an important presentation to win a client even though you are worried about getting it wrong. Or, it may be the opportunity to share an idea that could be rejected. Or, it may be hitting send on an email to a friend with whom you need to reconcile.

The difference-maker for you in your moment of testing is *bravery*.

If I had to choose one gift to impart upon every person I meet - one master key that unlocks their potential - it would be bravery. We need radical bravery in our workplaces, our schools, our neighborhoods, and - God help us - in our politics. If more people committed to making brave choices daily, we would see stronger, more effective teams, less corruption, less unhealthy conflict, and more progress on the societal issues that truly matter.

Organizations need leaders committed to cultivating a culture of bravery, and who themselves are making brave choices rather than cowering in self-protection. The marketplace needs more business owners who are willing to step up and do the right thing for their employees and their communities, even at the risk of personal cost. And, society needs more people to cultivate brave, empathetic relationships with people who think differently from them.

My ambition with this simple little book is to inspire an epidemic of everyday brave action. If you spend time considering the ideas and prompts within, you will learn the fundamental mechanics of rising to the moment instead of succumbing to it. You will learn how to lead others in a way that cultivates an environment of brave action. You will learn how to communicate in moments of uncertainty in a manner that unleashes the potential in others. You will discover how to infuse courage into everyday decisions.

You will develop the *habit* of bravery.

The word bravery tends to conjure images of storming beaches or running into buildings to save innocent victims. Yes, those acts are certainly brave! However, it's important to distinguish between *bravery* and *heroism*. While I probably wouldn't call you a hero for challenging your manager, doing so certainly requires bravery, especially when your job or organizational standing might be on the line. So while heroism is rising to an exceptional occasion, perhaps at risk of your own life, bravery is a habit that can be trained to prepare you for those everyday moments when your mettle is tested.

I believe that your best, strongest, and most contributive days are still ahead of you if you are willing to meet that test.

Will you *choose* brave?

Will you rise to the occasion, or be filled with regret?

Will you respond with bravery, or with *cowardice*?

For the record, I understand that the word coward is polarizing. It may be one of the worst things you can call someone. We don't celebrate cowards or write songs about them. Cowards are often shunned and expelled from positions of responsibility.

Cowards aren't considered *trust-worthy* because cowardice is choosing self-protection over doing the right thing. This means selling out your deeper aspirations for the sake of comfort, ease, and temporary reprieve from the uncertainty of the moment.

Cowardice is the very definition of selfishness, whereas bravery is self-less. While someone may appear brave to observers, if their actions are rooted in self-protection and selfish ambition, they may simply be acting boldly, but not bravely. Saying big words and making bold moves isn't necessarily brave if it's only to serve yourself.

And, this is why we don't trust cowards. We never know when their self-interests may become misaligned from ours and they'll throw us under the bus in order to protect themselves. They are not deemed worthy of trust, and even if we might find some alliance with them for a season of pursuing common ambitions, we are under no illusion that they are actually an ally.

I've spent most of my career working with professional problem-solvers. They go to work each day knowing that they will be confronting uncertainty, resolving difficult issues, inventing, designing, arguing, and presenting ideas to always critical and sometimes hostile audiences. These "creative professionals" often make leaps of intuition without a guarantee of success on the other side.

This requires bravery.

However, as many people progress in their career and have more to protect (reputation, income, relationships) they sometimes begin to shy away from big moments. They become more risk averse. They seek stability over challenge. They hoist their finger in the air to see which way the wind is blowing before making decisions.

Ironically, those with the most influence often become the most risk-averse. Every great organization began with someone taking a risk and creating something of value in spite of the odds. Then, once they have something to protect, many organizations huddle up, turn inward, and design their systems to protect what they've already done instead of seeking new frontiers to conquer. In my experience, this often happens because the key leadership has become disconnected from the core values that drove the organization to achieve greatness in the first place. They have lost sight of their first love.

Throughout *The Brave Habit* you will discover (a) what is worth taking a risk for, and (b) the price you are willing to pay for it. Your answers to these questions will determine whether or not you are poised for action when your moment comes.

COURAGE VS. BRAVERY

While courage is a popular topic these days, the discussion about it tends to feel inaccessible and impractical. It's like describing having vision, or being likable, or being smart. We all aspire to have these qualities, but how do we achieve them? For the purposes of this book, I will distinguish between courage and bravery. It's my belief that bravery is the *active* form of courage. Or, to put it a different way, courage is a resource at the ready, and bravery is the choice to deploy it in the moment of need.

As C.S. Lewis wrote, "Courage is not simply one of the

virtues but the form of every virtue at the testing point, which means at the point of highest reality. " It is at the testing point - in the moment of uncertainty - where we choose to deploy courage through brave action.

This means that bravery is a discipline rather than an inevitable outcome.

Bravery is not a personality trait, it's a decision you make. And, like any difficult thing that we choose to do in life, our capacity for acting bravely in important moments can be developed like a muscle. By practicing brave decisions in smaller, less consequential moments we train ourselves to be ready to act bravely when the stakes are higher.

Of course, "when the stakes are higher" is a relative term. What feels risky to one person may be commonplace to another. A bodybuilder will look at a 200 LB barbell and snicker, while to someone new to strength training it will pose a challenge. Sharing an outlier idea in a meeting or to a client might seem like an overwhelmingly risky thing to one person while feeling like an afterthought to another.

Each person's perception of risk is different, which means that brave action cannot be objectively measured. And, as the perception of risk shifts for a person, so does the definition of "brave".

When I was in my early twenties, I was terrified to speak in public. For some reason, each time I attempted to share an idea it felt like someone was grabbing my tongue and confusing my thoughts. I was so afraid of getting it wrong that I couldn't think clearly enough to get it right.

Something shifted for me when I was in my early thirties. I had experienced enough public speaking moments - and failed enough - to understand that the risk was nowhere near what I imagined. I even came to enjoy opportunities to teach. After getting my "reps" in for several years, I now routinely speak dozens of times per year to crowds of thousands of people at a time. It's one of my favorite things to do. I've even spoken to hundreds of thousands of people at once.

So, when I was in my twenties, stepping into a room of twenty people and delivering a talk was an act of bravery. Now, stepping onto a big stage and speaking to five thousand people isn't, because my perception of risk has shifted greatly.

Your calculation of bravery will change as you grow in wisdom and experience, which means that in order to continue growing you have to find new ways of developing the brave habit.

Throughout this book, you will be challenged to see small moments throughout your day as opportunities to engage in brave action.

For example:

• You don't want to speak up in a meeting and share an idea because you are concerned about how others might receive it, or about whether or not the idea is good enough to be introduced. At the heart of this is a desire to protect your reputation, but that may come at the expense of the team's work and the overall pool of ideas it has to choose from.

• When others start talking negatively about a teammate, you initially have a twinge of conscience that prompts you to either stem the conversation or just leave. However, you're concerned about how it might look to others if you walk away, and you don't want to come across as "too good" for everyone else, so you just go along with the group.

• While you regularly have flashes of insight and intuition that you want to follow, it's easier to just do work that doesn't raise any alarms or challenge any conventions. The net result is that you produce work that's good enough, but certainly not reflective of the kind of work that you could probably do if you were willing to take a few risks from time to time.

• Your relationship with your partner has been growing stagnant for a long time, and you both know (even if you won't acknowledge it) that the status quo can't hold forever. However, you've both settled into a pattern that's comfortable to both of you and you don't really fight much. So, rather than rocking the boat by having a pointed conversation about the trajectory of the relationship, you simply allow things to coast along.

• You have a product (or book/essay/design) that's been sitting in a drawer for months, but it never seems like it's the right time to share it with the world. You were initially very excited about it, but lately you've been talking yourself out of sharing it because it just doesn't have the same shine that it initially did. You convince yourself that it's probably not that good anyway, and that it would just be a waste of time to share it with others.

Any and all of these examples are moments when you choose comfort over cause, intent over action, cowardice over bravery.

Am I telling you that you should always share an idea when you have it, or that you should always take it upon yourself to correct the group when they are talking about a teammate? Of course not. However, those moments, as insignificant as they may seem at the time, are vector-changing with regard to your character.

ACTION AND CONSEQUENCE

You are a person of consequence.

What I mean by that is that the way in which you move, choose, act, and interact has a profound impact on the world around you. Over time, these choices add up to a lifetime of consequence. Each little choice, or "delta" (change) may seem insignificant in the moment, but in aggregate they form a body of work that stands as a testament to your time on this planet.

What will that body of work say about you? Will it represent you well, or will you one day wish that you'd stepped up to meet someone's moment of need, pushed a little harder to make a dent in the world around you, or taken a strategic risk to share that burning idea?

It's important to understand that nothing you do or choose

happens in isolation. In fact, almost every action you take or choice you make has a lingering impact on the world around you, and over time the impacts of those actions are exponential. There are people you will never meet who will be impacted by the choices you make.

An old proverb states that "A society grows great when old men (or women) plant trees in whose shade they know they will never sit." I would amend this proverb to say "A community achieves its potential when each person acts as if their choices have a permanent and lasting impact." A community can be a team, a family, a neighborhood, a country, or any group connected loosely by a common goal. As we benefit from the brave choices of others we are each granted an extra measure of assurance that brave action is possible for us as well.

Bravery yields more bravery.

Over time, a community's identity becomes defined by its bravery quotient. You raise the expectations within your sphere of influence every time you make a brave choice.

You convict others when you act on your own convictions.

This is especially important to note if you lead a team. They are taking their cues from your behavior and choices, and when you consistently shrink from the moment, they will take the hint that bravery is optional. When you consistently rise to the moment, they will take note that bravery is the expected norm. Your choices are amplified exponentially by your leadership responsibilities.

Now that we've framed up why each choice you make is an indispensable part of your larger body of work, let's begin to look at how to develop your capacity to make brave choices every day.

What does bravery even *mean*?

How can you tell if you are acting wisely or cowardly?

What is the difference between mere bravado and true bravery?

And perhaps most importantly, how can you develop the capacity for brave action in the face of uncertainty?

Bravery yields *more* bravery. You convict others when you act on your own convictions.

CHAPTER TWO

THE HERO MYTH

"To dare is to lose one's footing momentarily. To not dare is to lose oneself."

— SØREN KIERKEGAARD

For the remainder of the book, this will be our working definition of bravery:

Bravery is doing the right thing even in the face of fear or personal loss.

Not in the absence of fear or potential for loss, but in the face of it. Acting bravely means understanding the cost of failure, but choosing to do the right thing regardless.

Cowardice, on the other hand, is choosing self-protection over right action. Interestingly, it is possible to appear brave to others while actually behaving in a cowardly way. Someone can posture their decision as brave, but secretly be operating selfishly. This isn't bravery, it's just boldness. Inversely, you may appear a coward to others while actually doing the *brave* thing. Others may not always know your internal considerations, and may filter your actions through their own biases. Bravery is an intensely personal choice.

Bravery is doing the right thing, as best you know it, even when it's the uncomfortable thing. There's no discomfort involved in doing what's safe. It doesn't disrupt your standard of living, and it doesn't affect your relationships in any way. The brave choice is often marked with discomfort, awkward conversations, or misunderstandings from others. Don't expect that your bravery will always be celebrated. Others may not appreciate your choices because they don't understand *why* you made them.

Bravery is a choice, not a foregone conclusion. It's tempting to believe that bravery is a baked-in personality trait of certain individuals because this belief excuses cowardice. (I couldn't help it - it's just my nature!) However, bravery is a choice, and it's a response that can be trained like a muscle. As your tolerance for uncertainty increases, your response begins to reflect your values rather than your fears and anxiety. Acting with bravery does not make you a superhuman, it makes you fully human.

Bravery is always empathetic. It's not about you. If it was, then there is no real potential sacrifice involved. Brave action is always about the other. The other might be a person or a core principle that you hold dear, but the brave person is always looking outward when deciding. The coward only looks inward and to his own interests.

Bravery is action in spite of fear. People who choose to act bravely experience fear and insecurity as much as everyone else. It's just that they have developed the ability to choose cause over comfort.

Bravery is the willingness to fail in the pursuit of what matters. Just because you act bravely doesn't mean that you will get the results you want. However, the choice to do what's right supersedes the end result. In the end, your character will be formed more by *how* and *why* you made critical decisions in your life than by what those decisions yielded.

What bravery is not:

Bravery is not stupid risk. Closing your eyes and rolling the dice is not bravery. In fact, it may be the most cowardly thing you can do because it absolves you of the responsibility of your decision. A brave person counts the cost, and decides to act because the cost of inaction is simply too much to bear. Brave action is calculated risk in the face of uncertainty, not bold, brash decision-making.

Bravery is not bravado. Many people put bluster ahead of action. They posture and pretend they are acting bravely, but in truth they are only acting selfishly. However, brave people do not feel the need to posture. Instead, they allow their actions to speak for themselves. They are fine being misunderstood, and even disliked, if that's the cost of right action. They are willing to stand against the tide, on principle, even when others don't understand or follow.

Bravery is not for a select few. There are opportunities to be brave everywhere and every day. The need for bravery is in the workplace, in the home, in relationships, in neighborhoods, and everywhere humans interact.

Bravery is not impulsive. While brave actions often happen in a flash, the source of those actions are deeply-held beliefs about right and wrong, and a vision for a better future. Brave people are *realistic optimists*. While their decisions may appear impulsive, they are actually rooted in a deep connection to their values and ambitions. They are poised to act bravely because they have practiced the habit of bravery consistently.

Bravery is not anonymous or a remote action. Lobbing insults or attacks on someone from afar is not bravery. Labeling, irresponsibly accusing, and bandwagon-jumping in order to troll or mock someone is amongst some of the most cowardly behavior occurring in modern culture. Stepping into their world, looking them in the eye, and learning to love what you don't understand is the very definition of bravery.

THE CONDITIONS FOR BRAVERY

If bravery is a discipline, we have the moment by moment opportunity to develop our capacity for acting bravely. We can train our instincts to respond with a bias toward proactive response instead of self-protective reaction. As we will explore later, this doesn't necessarily mean that action is always warranted. Sometimes the bravest thing is actually to wait, or defer, or to continue to evaluate in the face of intense peer pressure to act. Regardless of whether bravery means acting or waiting, you can train yourself to respond with purpose.

A key requirement for brave action is uncertainty. If outcomes were guaranteed, there would be no need for bravery.

If you were *certain* that putting a thousand dollars into a company would yield a ten-fold return in five years, you'd be foolish not to do it.

If you were *certain* that your business idea would thrive and provide for your needs for decades to come, you'd already be doing it.

If you were *certain* that your idea would be well-received, you would have already written the proposal and presented it to your manager.

But, if these were certainties, everyone else would be doing them too.

Life is a universe of probabilities, not certainties. This means that we cannot seek certainty before we act. Instead, we must cultivate *clarity*.

Each person has a worldview out of which they form narratives to make sense of what's happening around them. If your worldview is clouded by the belief that bad results are inevitable, that effort is hopeless, and that any attempt to right wrongs is ultimately futile, you will tend toward self-protection because you feel your efforts to change things would be useless anyway. On the other hand, if your worldview is generally more optimistic and empowering with a belief that even small acts can cause larger long-term benefits to your organization or the larger community, you are more likely to engage in behavior that, while uncomfortable, may yield long-term benefits to you and the world around you.

To develop the brave habit, you must develop (1) clarity about what you are aspiring towards, and (2) understanding of what you're willing to do in order to achieve it. These are the two conditions that lead to brave action.

Bravery exists when we have a vision for a better possible future, and we trust that we have agency to help bring it about.

Consider the illustration below. On one axis, you have Perceived Agency versus Perceived Powerlessness. This means a belief that you have the ability to act in the face of uncertainty versus simply being resigned to your fate. On the other axis is Optimistic Vision about the future versus Pessimism about likely outcomes.

When you cultivate both the qualities of Optimistic Vision and Agency, the likelihood that you will make brave decisions in a moment of uncertainty grows.

And on teams, when each of these conditions exist it's more likely that members will make brave decisions for the sake of the organization's mission.

HIGH PERCEIVED AGENCY

NIHILISM / FUTILITY   **BRAVERY!**

PESSIMISM   OPTIMISTIC VISION

RESIGNATION   VICTIMHOOD

LOW PERCEIVED AGENCY

THE COWARDICE QUADRANTS

When either Optimism or Perceived Agency is lacking, you are likely to experience the temptation of cowardice.

High Perceived Agency, Pessimism = Nihilism/Futility

When you believe that you have the ability to act, but lack a clear vision of a better possible future, the situation feels hopeless. Yes, you have the skills and platform to do something, but you believe that even if you do act it's unlikely to change things and your effort would be wasted.

I often encounter sentiment like this inside of large organizations where mid-level employees feel helpless to change the cultural problems that plague the larger company. I hear things like, "Sure, I could try to alter the way our team interacts, but why would I? After all, that's just the way it is around here." This is a classic case of the absence of an optimistic vision of the way things *could* be.

Similarly, you might feel that you have the skills and a platform to pursue your ambitions, but you don't yet have a clear vision of how you'd like to deploy them, or to what end. In this situation, you need to become more clear about your vision for a better possible future. We will discuss how in chapter four.

Low Perceived Agency, Pessimism = Resignation

When you lack both a sense of optimism about a better possible future and a sense of agency to bring it about, you are resigned to your fate. You are simply drifting with the currents, and feel unable to do anything about it. You are simply being carried along to your destination.

For a few recent years, headlines about "quiet quitting" dominated magazines and journals as employers tried to figure out why team members were slacking while still collecting a paycheck. My hypothesis? They felt (a) pessimistic about their future prospects, and (b) that they didn't have any ability to influence the organization. So, they were resigned (without resigning.) What might it look like instead if their manager had understood this matrix and made an effort to paint a clearer vision of possibility for them, and/or equipped them with a greater degree of agency to bring about positive change? It may have completely changed their sense of engagement, and instead of taking the cowardly route of abdicating their responsibility they may have stepped up and re-engaged.

Low Perceived Agency, Optimistic Vision = Victimhood

When you have a vision for a better possible future, but lack a sense of agency to bring it about, you are in the quadrant of victimhood. You feel powerless to do anything about what you are experiencing, and have surrendered yourself to the powers that be.

To be clear, I'm not talking about victimization. There are very real victims in this world, and we must do all we can to help and support them. Rather, I'm talking about the mindset of victimization, in which we yield our ambitions because we don't believe we have the ability to pursue them. We'll discuss how to cultivate a sense of agency in chapter three.

High Perceived Agency, Optimistic Vision = Bravery

When we have a clear vision of a better possible future, and we believe we have the ability to help bring it about, this is the fertile field within which brave action is *likely* to occur. Please note that it doesn't mean bravery *will* occur. Rather, it's an environment in which those who are prepared to act are much more likely to do so.

As leaders, as storytellers, and as citizens we have a tremendous role to play in cultivating an environment in which people around us believe in a better possible future, and trust that they can do something to help bring it about. In order to do this, we must develop the brave habit.

THE BRAVE HABIT

In her book *The Creative Habit*, choreographer Twyla Tharp describes her discipline of going to her studio space for an early morning workout each day. She notes that while the end activity is working out in her space, that's not the actual ritual that she engages in daily.

She writes, "I wake up at 5:30 A.M., put on my workout clothes, my leg warmers, my sweatshirts, and my hat. I walk outside my Manhattan home, hail a taxi, and tell the driver to take me to the Pumping Iron gym at 91st street and First Avenue, where I work out for two hours.

"The ritual is not the stretching and weight training I put my body through each morning at the gym; the ritual is the cab. The moment I tell the driver where to go I have completed the ritual.

"It's a simple act, but doing it the same way each morning habitualizes it—makes it repeatable, easy to do. It reduces the chance that I would skip it or do it differently. It is one more item in my arsenal of routines, and one less thing to think about."

Even though the workout is Tharp's goal, hailing the cab is the *ritual*. It's what sets in motion the rest of the activity that leads to her desired results.

If you ultimately want to choose brave action more consistently, your aim begins with a simple ritual. While not quite as simple as the act of hailing a cab, it's a process that you can follow consistently to ensure that you are staying focused and active in the face of uncertainty, and that you are keeping action at the forefront rather than passively waiting for life to happen to you.

Please note the use of the word process. This is not as simple as "just do 10 reps with a dumbbell". Rather, through the regular use of self-reflection, centering on productive passion, and creative problem solving you can position yourself to seize the moment when it arises.

"Fortune favors the brave" is a Latin proverb that you've likely heard at some point. But what does it really mean?

Here's my re-phrasing: "Fortune favors those who prepare themselves for brave action."

There is a very simple five-part ritual that comprises the brave habit. By exercising this habit weekly you prepare yourself to seize your moment. To make the habit more memorable, I've managed to make the five steps spell the word BRAVE.

1. **Block** time for reflection. It might seem as if this is an obvious step, but it's really not. If something matters in life, we make time for it. Block off fifteen predictable minutes each week to engage in the brave habit. It could be at the very beginning of the week or at the end, but the important thing is that it's regular, predictable, and non-negotiable.

2. **Review** your life and work. A key reason why many people feel overwhelmed is that they haven't taken the time to define the

open questions and uncertainties that they are actually facing. They drift from day to day, but never make the intentional effort to identify what's giving them anxiety. Look at your upcoming meetings, tasks, projects, and conversations and consider what acting bravely might look like for you in each of them. Where do you feel uncertain and know that you will be required to act bravely?

What uncertainties am I facing right now? List 2-3 areas where brave action may be required in the coming days.

3. Take **Agency**. Decide what actions, big or small, you will take this week in order to confront the uncertainty that you are facing. What do you know and what *don't* you know? Where do you need to seek clarity? What questions should you be asking, but have been avoiding? What skill could you be developing to prepare for upcoming challenges? What small, brave actions could you take in the coming days to give you a sense of progress on your important priorities?

What agency can I leverage in each of those areas to affect change? What is an acceptable risk for each area? What is an unacceptable risk?

4. **Visualize** your better possible future. Re-root yourself in why you do what you do, who you are serving, and your deeper sense of productive passion. (More about this in chapter four.) What is worth the risk? Remind yourself of what you value so that it's top of mind as you make decisions throughout your week.

What is my vision for a better possible future in each of my areas of responsibility?

5. **Express** your intent and mission for the week. What does it look like to make brave choices this week?

What brave next action can I take today? And, who will hold me accountable?

In the next two chapters, we'll explore how to develop your sense of Optimistic Vision, and how to cultivate Perceived Agency. If you'd like to see where you might fall on the matrix displayed earlier in the chapter, you can take the Brave Index to discover your Brave Quotient.

Visit **TheBraveHabit.com** to take the index and receive a customized action plan based on your results.

In the moment of uncertainty, what you *truly* believe is revealed.

CHAPTER THREE

CULTIVATING AGENCY

CHOOSING ACTION OVER INTENT

"Inaction breeds doubt and fear. Action breeds confidence and courage. If you want to conquer the negative elements in your life, don't sit at home and think about it. Go out and get busy!"

— DALE CARNEGIE

PRINCIPLE: **To develop the brave habit you must cultivate a sense of agency to accomplish your goals and vision.**

As discussed in the last chapter, brave action is more likely to occur when (a) you believe in a better possible future, and (b) you believe you have the ability to bring it about. In this chapter we're going to discuss how to develop a sense of personal agency, or a confidence in your ability to influence the world around you.

In his 1989 book *The 7 Habits of Highly Effective People*, Stephen R. Covey introduced a concept he called the Circles of Concern and Influence. Your Circle of Concern is an expansive circle that contains everything in the world that occupies your attention, causes you to worry, or could affect you in some way. As Covey wrote, ""In the Circle of Concern are the wide range of concerns we have, such as our health, our children, problems at work, the national debt, nuclear war... There are some things over which we have no real control. We are deeply concerned about them, but we can only have a limited influence, if any, over them."

Your Circle of Influence is a much smaller circle that represents the area within which you can take agency and influence the world around you. "In the Circle of Influence are those things we can do something about," Covey wrote. "This includes our behaviors, our attitudes, and our efforts. We can work on our habits, work on being a more patient parent, or learn new skills to be more effective at work. In our Circle of Influence, we can directly affect change."

As you increase your sense of personal agency, your Circle of Influence grows as does your ability to shape the concerns that affect you. You begin to see the direct effect of brave action, which reinforces your sense of agency, and the entire cycle perpetuates.

However, as your sense of personal agency diminishes, your belief that brave action is possible can also shrink. This means that you become more cautious, seeing yourself as the victim of your circumstances rather than their shaper.

In his book *Nerve: Poise Under Pressure, Serenity Under Stress*, Taylor Clark cites post World War II research into combat stress among combatants. He wrote, "According to the 1945 report 'Men Under Stress,' the mortality rate for dogfighters was among the highest in the military; the pilots knew that half of them would be killed in action. Yet fighter pilots also enjoyed wildly high job satisfaction, with 93 percent of them claiming to be happy with their assignments. And why should they be so content? Because fighter pilots felt they were in complete control of their fate. They could maneuver however they liked through a huge airspace, and they believed, to a man, that their piloting skill would determine their survival, not luck."

This sense of satisfaction with their role can be summed up in one word: *agency*. While every single participant in the war understood the overall mission, some felt much more at the mercy of the military brass who were plotting their next move. For fighter pilots, there was a sense that their future was in their own hands - that they were the agents of their own fate - even though their role was among the most dangerous in the military.

In order to develop the brave habit, you must believe that you have your hand on the controls. To do this, develop a sense of Perceived Agency, meaning a belief that you have the ability to influence or bring about your vision.

The opposite of perceived agency is Perceived

Powerlessness. This means that while you may have clarity about a better possible future, you feel helpless to do anything to influence it. Thus, you are largely resigned to your fate.

Albert Bandura was one of the most influential psychologists of the past century. His work included decades of research into a concept that he called Self-Efficacy, or the self-perception of capability to influence the world around us. He wrote, "Perceived self-efficacy refers to beliefs in one's capabilities to organize and execute the courses of action required to produce given attainments." The effects of perceived self-efficacy are significant, especially in the face of uncertainty or danger. Bandura continued, "People's beliefs in their efficacy have diverse effects. Such beliefs influence the courses of action people choose to pursue, how much effort they put forth in given endeavors, how long they will persevere in the face of obstacles and failures, their resilience to adversity, whether their thought patterns are self-hindering or self-aiding, how much stress and depression they experience in coping with taxing environmental demands, and the level of accomplishments they realize."

According to Bandura, regardless of their desire, perceived self-efficacy is a critical factor in whether people act upon their goals, ambitions, and perceived opportunities. When there is low perceived self-efficacy, the individual is far less likely to extend themselves in the face of potential consequences. He concluded, "Beliefs of personal efficacy constitute the key factor of human agency. If people believe they have no power to produce results, they will not attempt to make things happen."

While Bandura's research highlights that a sense of agency is critical in the moment when brave action is required, that perceived agency is not theoretical or collective. It's highly individual. Each person must believe in their ability to bring about their desired change.

There are three primary categories of agency that you can develop in order to increase the likelihood of brave action: Proficiency (your skills and mindset), People (your relationships and ability to call on your network to get things done), and Platform (the influence that you are able to leverage to achieve your goal).

Proficiency

As you survey your current responsibilities, goals, and ambitions, what skills do you depend on to help you complete them? Do you have all of the skills you need, or are there outages? What skills do you need to develop to help you meet the challenges that lay ahead of you?

Your perception of your mastery of core skills is critical. The more practice you have, the more confidence you will develop in moments of uncertainty. For example, for many people the idea of playing an improvisational guitar solo is a mind-bending exercise in creativity. However, most accomplished guitarists have spent so many hours practicing the core techniques of their trade, playing scales forward and backward at varying speeds, and emulating other great players that when the time comes to perform a guitar solo they are able to draw from a deep library of possibilities, quickly evaluate them, and perform them seamlessly. They have developed core competence by practicing basic patterns over and over, which gives them confidence to take a chance on improvisational riffs.

The key with regard to mastery isn't that you perceive that you could do something with ease. Rather, it's that you believe that you have the ability to accomplish it, even if it is challenging. Phil Libin has founded multiple companies, including the very successful note taking platform Evernote. In an interview, he told me that the most valuable ideas to pursue are those that (a) have just become possible for the first time in human history, and (b) are still really difficult to accomplish. This means that while technically possible, very few people will pursue these ideas because of the difficulty involved. The willingness to look at such opportunities and say "it would be difficult, but I could do that if I chose to" is what we mean by a sense of agency.

Many people simply rely on their past successes to help them meet their present challenges, but eventually you will be outmatched. In order to position yourself for continual brave action, commit to continuous skill development. Here are a few questions to help you identify skills that you may want to consider adding to your development plan:

• Where do you feel the most insecure or "out of your league" in your daily life? Is it due to a skill that you lack or some kind of knowledge that you haven't attained?

• Have you ever hit a wall because you lacked the skill to take a project to the next level? What happened, and what would have allowed you to go farther?

• As you consider people you admire, what do they seem to have in abundance that you lack? How might you be able to develop it?

There's no magic formula to developing proficiency. It's simply a matter of committing to a plan, doing the hard work of developing that skill every day, and measuring your progress.

Action: Choose one skill that you are going to develop over the next three months. Then, choose a method for learning it (a course, workbook, mentor, etc.) and plot a plan of action. Measure your progress so that you know how you're doing along the way.

People

None of us work in a vacuum. We depend on others in order to achieve our goals, which means that our network is an essential element of our sense of agency. And, the deeper and more diverse our network, the more leverage we have over uncertainty because we are able to draw upon the expertise of others in our moment of need.

Do you intentionally seek and cultivate relationships with others in your life and work, or do you simply take relationships as they come? The people you surround yourself with are your deepest source of courage, and are also likely to be the ones to

41

provide perspective on when you should act and when you should wait. Seek to surround yourself with quality people of character.

- Do the people you spend the most time with encourage you to grow, or reinforce bad habits?
- Do you have people you can call upon for wisdom in a moment of uncertainty, or are you always the smartest person in the room?
- Do you regularly reach out to encourage others in your network, or are you solely on the receiving end of others' encouragement?

Action: Attend one networking event or work to cultivate a new relationship every quarter that helps you take action toward your vision of a better future.

Platform

It doesn't matter how brilliant your idea is if you have no platform from which to introduce it to the world. In fact, mediocre ideas introduced through an expansive platform will often outperform brilliant ideas introduced through a mediocre platform. So in order to increase your sense of agency, consider your platform.

While many people have great ideas, far fewer have the resources and opportunity to bring those ideas into the world. Fewer still are willing to leverage that platform - and all that it could cost to act - in order to see that change enacted.

In his book *Profiles In Courage*, former United States

president (and then United States senator) John F. Kennedy shared the stories of several politicians who expended significant political capital in order to support a cause they believed in, but that others in their political party stood opposed to. While many average citizens may have felt similarly about the issues at hand, only someone with the platform for action, such as a sitting U.S. senator, could act meaningfully to bring about that change.

In a similar manner, someone with greater authority within an organization has more capacity to act on opportunities than someone with a smaller platform. In examining your platform for action, consider the "capital" that you have to spend in order to see the results you want.

- Where have you earned trust that gives you the right to speak your ideas?
- What audience has given you permission to share with them?
- Which relationships have you developed that will happily circle around you as you pursue your vision?
- What resources have you garnered that can be spent on behalf of your cause?

The challenge is this: *as your platform grows, so does the perceived cost of action.* The stakes often feel much higher once you have something to protect.

Your platform is any area in which you have amplification, meaning your leadership role, your trusted relationship with a leader in your organization, your influence with your peers, or your standing in your community. The key is to grow your platform in a way that's consistent with your goals. While leading a neighborhood development project gives you a platform within your community, it will probably matter little at work. Make sure that you are developing your platform in ways that align with your vision of a better future.

•In what areas do you have outsized influence compared to your peers? How does that (or might that) platform give you agency to pursue your goals and vision?

•Where do you have more credibility than others, and how might you leverage it in order to pursue your vision of a better possible future?

Action: Determine which elements of your platform can be developed to give you better ability to pursue your vision.

By committing to continual growth and development of each of the "3 P's", you increase your likelihood of brave action in moments of uncertainty. Then, you must commit to turning your sense of agency into action.

FROM AGENCY TO ACTION

I've despised running for most of my life. After playing multiple sports in high school, all of which required a lot of running and conditioning, I swore off running as exercise for decades. Instead, I preferred to play sports like basketball, where at least my running had a purpose other than self-torture. When I was in my mid forties, I tore my ACL while playing in a pickup basketball game and my exercise options were suddenly very limited. After my recovery, I decided to give running one more try.

On my first run, I made it close to a half mile before I was bent over gasping for air. I turned around and walked home. The next time, I ran closer to a mile, very slowly. It felt like a huge accomplishment, even though you could have timed my pace with a calendar. This went on for months, as I developed my capacity for distance and speed. One day, as I was turning a corner and hitting mile three, something odd happened: I realized I was actually enjoying my run. I was lost in the moment, listening to a podcast, and was no longer fixated on how tortured I felt. Instead, running was just something I did. It had become a habit.

Now, any day on which I don't run feels strange. It feels like something is missing. The very thing I'd most despised for years had become an indispensable part of my routine.

The same principle holds true for bravery. We develop the capacity for acting bravely through the daily practice of making small, brave decisions. Every time we pause and act deliberately with bravery we increase our capacity to act bravely in the future. We make bravery a part of our identity and essential to how we see ourselves in the world.

Small, daily, decisive brave actions transform your perspective of bravery from an enormous act of will to a natural outcome of your identity. You begin to see yourself as someone who does brave things.

Bravery is proven through your actions, not your intentions. However, acting doesn't always mean *doing*. Sometimes acting can mean *not* doing, or *releasing* something you believe you are entitled to even though it hurts to do so.

THREE MODES OF BRAVERY

"Just do it - *now*!"

"Don't think. Just take the plunge."

"Act fast. Otherwise, you'll talk yourself out of it."

While well-intended, this advice is often brash and unwise. Bravery isn't just about what you do, it can sometimes be about what you choose not to do. As you develop the habit of bravery, you may choose to defer action because deferring is, in fact, the bravest choice in the moment.

There are three forms that brave choices might take.

Bravery To Act

This is bravery in its most obvious form. We think of people running into burning buildings, taking leaps of faith, or exposing corruption in a very public way. Those moments certainly require bravery. However, so do everyday decisions in which you must choose to do the right thing even at potential personal cost.

What are the qualities of brave action?

Brave people are protective, cowards exploit. If your actions are to protect someone or something vulnerable, whether a person or ideal, then there's a good chance it's the right action. Bravery, by its very nature, is protective of what it cares about and is compelled to protect and defend it. Bravery stands in the gap for the vulnerable.

Brave people reveal the truth at the right time, cowards conceal it. Brave people know that the truth is never really a threat, but even if it costs them their livelihood or relationship, the cost of inaction is simply too vast to take the easy way out. Bravery seeks truth, even when it's inconvenient.

Brave people consider context and scale, cowards think about right now. The brave choice is the one that takes into account nuance and context, is empathetic, and scales in a positive way. Cowardly action is only concerned with immediate consequences. Those who act bravely consider the larger context of their actions, not just their immediate results. Bravery seeks long-term viability, not instant gratification.

Brave people are principle-driven, cowards go with their gut. Brave people have a framework for making decisions that is so ingrained that their actions in the face of adversity are almost automatic. Cowards, on the other hand, simply react in the moment in order to protect themselves and their interests. Bravery is bounded by a belief in a greater principle.

Brave people face consequences, cowards blame others. Brave people are willing to be known by their choices, and are willing to face the consequences of their actions, whether good or bad. Brave people do not play the victim. Bravery takes accountability for its actions and beliefs. Cowards are never to blame, seek a scapegoat for every instance of failure, and throw people - even their allies - under the bus.

Brave people initiate, cowards just allow life to happen to them. Those who choose bravery know that it often means being the first-mover, when others are scared to do so. It means initiating reconciliation in a relationship. Being the first to start a venture. Being the first into the water. Bravery makes things happen rather than just letting things happen. Cowards just take things as they come, backward-rationalizing why what happened was exactly what they wanted anyway.

Brave people listen, cowards want to be heard. Brave people are not threatened by differing opinions. Brave leaders know that brilliance is forged in the cauldron of creative conflict. Bravery isn't threatened by disagreement. Cowards are more concerned with being seen as the driving force behind every idea than with the idea actually being effective and providing value.´

Brave people follow-through, cowards hedge. Those who choose brave action know that it means seeing things through to the end, even when it gets uncomfortable. Cowards might be eager to jump in, but abandon their effort when it costs them something. Bravery persists in the face of hardship.

The financial crisis of 2008-09 caught many people unaware, especially those who worked in the real estate industry. Scott was definitely in a bind. As a commercial real estate agent, he suddenly found his industry spiraling and it was looking increasingly likely he would be left without an income at the worst possible time - while expecting the birth of twins. With a family to support, his work was vanishing and Scott began to consider his options. He was offered a job selling office furniture, and while that path would provide a paycheck and a bit of stability to help his family through the difficult time, he also knew that he simply wasn't suited for the work. The other option that Scott began mulling over was to make the leap from commercial to residential real estate, leveraging his network to jumpstart his business. Even with his experience in commercial real estate, it was a big risk, especially with the market reeling as it was. "I knew I had the skills to be able to make it work," Scott told me, "but it was still a big unknown given what was happening with the economy." So much was out of his control.

In reviewing his options with his wife Kristen, Scott was leaning heavily toward taking the job selling office furniture. It was steady work, and it would give him some time to consider his next move. However, Kristen wasn't convinced. She told Scott that he simply wasn't wired for the repetitive nature of the sales job. She knew he would be miserable, and that either way the office furniture job would be a temporary fix. Together, they developed a plan for Scott to launch his residential real estate practice, but wisely set some rails and milestones for the venture. They cashed-in their investments and savings, which gave them about six months of runway before they would need to find another way to generate income. They decided that if there wasn't significant momentum at the six month mark, they would reconsider and Scott would take a salaried job.

For the first few months things were slow, but just in the nick of time Scott was able to get his first home under contract, generating a bit of income to extend their runway and show that the business might actually work. Over the coming months, Scott began to generate more and more income and - in spite of the economic conditions still not being ideal - he was able to build a sustainable residential real estate practice.

Over a dozen years later, Oyler-Hines is thriving, in the top ten of all Coldwell Banker teams in the United States. It's certainly not been a smooth ride, but Scott told me that when he was in the midst of his most challenging moments, trying to make a decision about what to do next, he kept returning to a quote from Dr. Rita Levi-Montalcini, "Above all, don't fear difficult moments. The best comes from them."

Of course, we love to celebrate stories of bravery like Scott's that work out in the end. But for a moment, pretend that Scott and Kristen had failed. Did they *still* make the right decision?

I believe they did, because **it's possible to make a good, brave decision that has a bad outcome.**

You cannot evaluate *past* decisions based upon your *present* understanding.

Regret is often the result of applying new learnings to past situations. As you grow, you become wiser, more experienced, and more mature in your ability to recognize patterns. So, it's natural to have a twinge of regret when you consider the past. It may even cause you to double-think your present decisions, not because you're trying to do what's right but because you're trying to avoid doing what's wrong. I call this dynamic "retro-analysis paralysis".

Either an inability to move due to fear of getting it wrong, or a knee-jerk reaction to bad outcomes in the past can prevent you from choosing bravely in the present moment. It robs you of your sense of agency.

The qualities of brave action in this section are filters through which you can sift your own decisions.

Am I initiating, or deferring?

Am I listening, or do I just want to be heard?

Am I operating out of principle, or just going with my gut?

Brave action is the most obvious manifestation of bravery, but it can also take two additional forms.

Bravery To Let Go

When I was five years old, I had an inescapable crush on a girl in my grade. I wanted so desperately for her to notice me, but all of the other boys were constantly showering her with attention and I simply couldn't compete. One day at recess, an inspired plan came to me in a flash: I would climb to the top of the tallest set of monkey bars, then in front of everyone I would swing upside down, back and forth by my legs and shout her name.

What girl could *possibly* resist such an act of skill and charm?

It was only a few minutes before recess ended, so I had to move quickly. I climbed the bars, made my way out to the middle, secured my legs and let my body fall backward while simultaneously yelling "Hey Jenny! Look at me!"

Unfortunately, in my feverish determination to get Jenny's attention, I'd not heard the recess bell. Everyone on the playground was lined up in complete silence a short distance away, already prepared to go back inside, and I was swinging upside down in front of them proclaiming my love to the world. First, the giggles started. Then, the laughs. Finally, the mimicking shouts of "Hey Jenny!"

Worse, while I had a good plan to get up onto the monkey bars, I had no plan for getting back down. I managed to maneuver until I was hanging by my hands, but couldn't generate enough momentum to swing to the next bar. I was stuck until my teacher lifted me by the waist and placed me on the ground. It took weeks for the snickering to end, and Jenny never reciprocated my affection. But the worst part of it all was that I'd put myself in a situation that I simply couldn't get out of. That early experience affected me in such a way that it was years before I could show my interest in another girl. I was stuck in that moment of embarrassment.

Obviously, I eventually moved on and most of my friends completely forgot about the incident, but it still stings just a little even to this day. Oddly, the context of my shame was closely related to a principle that I later came to learn is critical to both human development and developing the habit of bravery: **brachiation**.

Brachiation is a term used both in zoology and in childhood development to describe the ability to swing from one hold to another. For example, think of a child who is playing on a set of "monkey bars". The child must master the ability to let go of one bar while simultaneously grabbing ahold of another. Fear of falling is often the root cause of the inability to brachiate. After all, if the next grip isn't secure, the trip to the ground will be rapid and unforgiving. Ironically, if the child is unable - or unwilling - to let go, momentum will be stalled and the child will get stuck in the middle. This inevitably means falling anyway, or screaming for someone to come and rescue them.

While most adults have mastered physical brachiation, psychological brachiation can be much more difficult to embrace. Much like the fearful child on the monkey bars, when we lack the ability to let go of the way things have been and move on to something new, we get stuck. We stall our momentum. While we may not be in physical harm, we spend months or years spinning our wheels, hopelessly stuck in place, unable to move forward. In our desire to maintain stability by remaining rooted in the present/past, we undermine our future potential.

Imagine standing with one foot securely on shore, and one foot in a boat. For a while, you can have both the safety of the shore and the freedom of the boat. However, once the boat begins to separate from the shore you must make a decision: either stay on the shore where it's safe, predictable, and secure, or jump in the boat and embrace the adventure and potential risk. If you try to remain half and half, you'll end up in the water.

Often, the reason we fail to let go of the present/past is because it's simply too comfortable for us. We may not like our present circumstances, but at least they are familiar to us. They pose no immediate threat. Our understanding of our identity is wrapped up in what we have accomplished, how others perceive us, and our perceived or desired role in the world.

We would rather live with perceived invulnerability than to test our limits and discover we actually have some.

Sometimes the act of bravery that's required of us is bravery to let go. We must be willing to appreciate and value what has already been while simultaneously embracing what might be, giving that our full attention and effort. Sometimes, we must let go even before we've fully secured our grip on the next bar.

This can be difficult, especially if you've been deeply in pursuit of a goal or dream that didn't work out the way you'd hoped. Much of your sense of identity can become wrapped up in pursuing a *thing*, and when it doesn't work out, the emotional labor necessary to separate yourself from that dream can be overbearing. This is why so many people still live in the past - retelling old stories, revisiting the "glory days". They haven't fully let go of what used to be and embraced what now is. They are still sorting out their identity apart from their past accomplishments or relationships.

However, if you are unwilling to let go of the past, you will inevitably get stuck in the present and will be unable to meet the needs of the future. Optimizing around what's most comfortable is a guaranteed way to find yourself incapable of meeting the demands of tomorrow. Training yourself to experience small amounts of discomfort daily will prepare you for the moments when you are asked to do something that feels like a risk.

Many organizations experience a similar dynamic when they go through times of change or restructuring. While the new systems might be more efficient and better for the team long-term, in the near-term there are always team members who prefer to hang onto the existing ways of doing things because those processes are more comfortable and familiar at the moment. There is a kind of "letting go" that has to happen for the team to move forward, but many are reluctant to do so. A part of the leader's responsibility is to paint a picture of a better possible future, and to help the team understand that the new processes are the method to achieve that vision. In other words, to cultivate an environment in which the team can be brave enough to let go of the way things were and embrace the way things could be.

I have the opportunity to talk with many very accomplished people, such as business leaders, artists, and writers. Most outside observers think that there is probably a singular moment when they felt like they'd "made it" or when success finally arrived. However, when I ask these very successful people about that moment I often hear things like "there wasn't really *one* moment, there was a string of them" or "it just happened over time" or "it snuck up on me." This has reinforced a belief that I've long had that success doesn't come all at once, but instead comes in layers. By the time you achieve the success you've long desired, it's likely to just feel like the next logical step in a long series of steps you've been taking to that point.

The same is true of risk. While we often think that bravery is about taking giant leaps into the unknown, in reality a brave decision often feels a bit commonplace to those who are making it because they've trained themselves over time to see risk as a natural part of what it means to do valuable work.

As you survey your life, is there any place where you simply need to exercise the bravery to let go and move on? Are you holding onto the bar too long, in danger of falling because you're unwilling to act bravely?

Bravery To Wait

There's a more subtle form of brave action that in some ways looks like *inaction* - bravery to wait. Sometimes the most brave decision you can make is to stand firm against the tide, even when everything around you is trending in the other direction. You may feel like you're missing out on a golden opportunity, or others may tell you that you are foolish to pause, but you know deep down that it's not the right time. Your particular act of bravery is to stand against popular opinion or critique.

In fact, there will be times in your life and leadership when it seems like you are the only person who *doesn't* think something is a good idea. Now, it's always possible that you're missing some key piece of information that would prove you wrong. However, it's also possible that the timing just isn't right... *yet*.

In these moments, the bravest thing you can do is stand with your feet firmly planted, even as the tide is rushing against you and everyone around you is telling you that you are foolish. Note that this is not an excuse for cowardly inaction. I'm not telling you that you should sit on the sidelines because you don't want the discomfort of being in the midst of the action. Rather, it's an acknowledgement that action in and of itself is not necessarily brave. Sometimes it's merely bold.

We often celebrate stories of successful entrepreneurs who cast caution to the wind and brashly launched a business before they should have. However, we often suffer from survivorship bias, a term used to describe a cognitive trap in which we generalize the traits or outcomes of a small group to the general population. So, because the stories of successful risk-takers are celebrated, we generally think that success means taking wild leaps of faith.

Of course you've heard of those phenomenally successful entrepreneurs! Their stories grace the cover of every magazine. What you don't often hear about are the unfortunate souls who also leaped before they should have and failed miserably either due to poor timing, poor resources, or a general lack of skill and platform to bolster success. Maybe they were so afraid of missing out on an opportunity that they couldn't muster the courage to wait until they were truly ready to seize it. Maybe they acted not out of true bravery, but out of a kind of cowardice that fears being mocked for missing the moment.

This is why patience is often its own form of bravery.

Patience requires you to quiet the deeper impulse to leap blindly in favor of a more strategic course of action. This isn't an excuse not to act, but is instead permission to act in strategic ways while you ready yourself for the bigger risk. One of the ways you prepare is by growing your network of truth-tellers.

I was once speaking at a large event for the US Air Force, and a retired four-star general was among the other speakers. As I was in the green room eating a blueberry muffin, he quietly approached from behind and when I turned around I was face to face with this legendary military leader. He asked my advice about creativity, then I asked him what he considered the most important thing leaders should know. Without hesitating, he replied "You need people around you to speak truth to you before you realize you need people around you to speak truth to you. By the time you realize you need them, it's already too late."

If you only seek people to tell you what you want to hear, you'll definitely attract them. You can always find someone to encourage you to take a foolish leap into the unknown. They probably don't really care about you, they just want to see what happens!

Don't fall prey to the myth that bravery means rash action. The reality is often the opposite. The person standing silently and observantly on the sidelines, while often mistaken for a coward, might be surveying the game and waiting for the perfect moment to pounce.

Is there any place in your life or work where you feel compelled to take a wild leap into the unknown, and may even feel fear of missing out if you don't? Would that leap be true bravery, or mere boldness and bravado?

We enact our sense of agency by making brave choices in the moment of uncertainty. Whether it's through acting, letting go, or waiting, bravery is proven through what we *do* not what we *intend*. However, agency alone is not enough to inspire brave action. In the next chapter, we'll dive deeper into how to cultivate an optimistic vision of the future.

CHECKPOINT:

It's important to remember that bravery isn't just about bold action. For this season of your life, consider the following questions:

• What brave action have you been deferring because you don't believe you have the agency to act? How might you commit to developing the skills, platform, or relationships you need to act?

• Is there anything you simply need to let go of right now? What is it, and what does letting go look like?

• Is there any place in your life where bravery right now means waiting? What does this mean for you, and what potential negative feedback could that elicit from those around you?

CHAPTER FOUR

CULTIVATING OPTIMISTIC VISION

PURSUING CAUSE OVER COMFORT

"The pessimist complains about the wind; the optimist expects it to change; the realist adjusts the sails."

— WILLIAM ARTHUR WARD

PRINCIPLE: **To develop the brave habit, root yourself in a vision of a better possible future and cultivate optimism.**

It is impossible to pursue comfort and great work simultaneously. You can experience comfort while pursuing great work, but you cannot chase both at the same time. All of the easy things have been done, so the pursuit of worthwhile goals requires that you do the hard things that few others are willing to attempt.

What fuels a willingness to continually step out of your comfort zone? A belief that your effort will be worth it.

OPTIMISM AND PASSION

Martin Seligman is known by many as the father of the positive psychology movement. His research into learned helplessness, optimism, and agency are foundational to our modern understanding of how humans overcome adversity. According to Seligman, optimism is a linchpin ingredient for societal progress. Throughout human history, from the age of hunter-gatherer through the advent of agriculture, the Industrial Revolution, and the modern age of technological revolution, the key driver of progress has been a belief that a better future is possible.

Optimists believe that challenging circumstances are temporary (not hopelessly permanent), local (as in, not universal in their life), and changeable (as in, they can do something now or in the future to make them better). On the other hand, those who default to learned helplessness tend to believe that circumstances are permanent, pervasive, and personal (meaning that they were due to the individual's unique lack of some valuable quality rather than being random).

According to Seligman's research, optimists tend to try harder, and become better or faster when under pressure. They also tend to be more innovative and creative than their less agency-minded peers when faced with adversity. Most surprisingly, they tend to be healthier over time, living on average six to eight years longer than those who live with a mindset of learned helplessness.

What this means is that developing an optimistic mindset is not only critical to your ability to develop the brave habit, but it also carries tremendous psychological and health benefits as well. According to Seligman, those who exist in the bottom quartile of optimism experience health effects that are equivalent to smoking *two to three packs of cigarettes a day!*

So, if optimism is critical to the belief that we can create change in the world, how do we develop it?

THE KEY TO OPTIMISTIC VISION

The most predictable driver of optimism is *productive* passion. This is an outcome that you care so deeply about that you are willing to suffer if necessary to achieve it. It is clean fuel.

As Kierkegaard wrote, "Cowardice settles deep in our souls like the idle mists on stagnant waters. From it arise unhealthy vapors and deceiving phantoms. The thing that cowardice fears most is decision; for decision always scatters the mists, at least for a moment. Cowardice thus hides behind the thought it likes best of all: the crutch of time."

In *Die Empty* I wrote about what I call the "passion fallacy". We toss around phrases like "follow your passion" as if it means simply pursuing things that you enjoy. On the surface, there's nothing wrong with this advice except for the fact that we are fundamentally mis-using the word "passion". In its root form, the word passion comes from the Latin word *passio* which means "to endure or suffer". When we encourage someone to follow their passion, what we're really saying is "follow your suffering!" (Doesn't quite have the same ring to it, huh?)

This fundamental twist of the common advice about passion is something I can get fully behind, because it's the foundation of brave action. When you tap deeply into a productive passion, it means that you are willing - if necessary - to suffer if necessary in order to achieve an outcome that matters more to you than your temporary discomfort. It doesn't mean that you necessarily *will* suffer, only that you're willing to do so in order to achieve your vision.

If you are pursuing a worthy vision, and you are driven by confident ambition, you will at times experience suffering. Discomfort. Failure, in ways big and small. To continue to cultivate brave action, stay rooted in your productive passion. Understand the deeper why of your pursuit.

When you have a clear vision of what matters deeply to you and of the person you want to be, that clarity cuts like a knife between bravery and cowardice. In moments of testing, your decision to do the right thing, even when it's uncomfortable, becomes more bearable.

On December 20, 1943, an American bomber *Ye Olde Pub* was severely damaged on its return from a bomb run over an aircraft factory in Bremen, Germany. After flak hit the plane, damaging it and forcing it to slow down and leave its formation, the B-17, piloted by 2nd Lt. Charlie Brown, was attacked by more than a dozen German fighters. The plane was so damaged that the crew discussed the possibility of simply ditching it in the nearest clearing and taking their chances in the German countryside. With one crew member dead and many severely injured, they decided to take their chances and attempt to fly the plane back to friendly airspace.

Unfortunately for the crew, the damaged plane was spotted by German troops on the ground. A German pilot, Franz Stigler, was soon airborne to intercept the struggling B-17 and shoot it down. Stigler caught up to the plane and assumed the attack position. The American pilot Brown later indicated that he knew they were certain to be shot down by the German pilot. However, once Stigler got close enough to see the damage, he could tell that the crew posed no threat, and through holes in the fuselage he could see the extent of the injuries onboard. Stigler flew alongside the bomber and attempted to persuade them to land on a German airstrip and surrender, but Brown's crew couldn't understand his signals, opting to continue flying toward friendly airspace. In a surprising twist, Stigler flew close off of the bomber's wing so as to prevent German guns from shooting the American plane down as it made its way to safety.

Upon reaching safe territory, to the surprise of everyone on *Ye Olde Pub*, Stigler gave a salute to the American bomber crew and flew off. The crew was so surprised and skeptical of Stigler's motives that Brown instructed his gunner to continue to target Stigler's plane until it was out of sight. They navigated the plane safely to a British airfield, saving all of the crew but the one who had been killed in the initial attack. In the years after the incident, Charlie Brown would recall the story of the unexpected German escort to audiences at post-war events, and offered that he wished he could someday have the chance to meet the other pilot. One day, he received a letter claiming to be from the German pilot, and after corroborating some of the lesser-known details of the events, he confirmed that Franz Stigler was indeed the pilot who had ensured the safe return of the bomber. The two remained close friends over the decades leading up to their deaths.

When asked why he chose to protect the American bomber rather than shoot it down, Stigler echoed the words of an early commanding officer from when he was stationed in North Africa. The officer told him "If I ever see or hear of you shooting at a man in a parachute, I will shoot you myself." Stigler said that the condition on *Ye Olde Pub* was no different than being in a parachute, because the plane was completely defenseless. Years later, those words from his early commander still framed up how he viewed his role as a fighter pilot. In that moment , even though his current commanding officer sent him up with the expectations that he would shoot the plane down, he chose to do what he thought was right regardless of the potential consequences he might face upon his return. His framework for making that decision had been cemented years before.

Now, if it's possible for you to suspend your knowledge of

which side each person was fighting for, and also remove yourself from any judgment about the justifications of war or the weight of its atrocities, consider the following about the decision that Stigler made that day:

- His peers on the ground certainly knew that he had spotted the bomber and had taken off in his plane in order to chase it down.
- Anti-aircraft guns on the ground could almost certainly see that he - a German pilot - was escorting an American bomber so as to prevent it from being shot at. That was the entire reason he flew so close to the bomber to begin with.
- The year - 1943 - was a critical year for both sides in the war, and any concession by either side could tilt the balance, at least psychologically.
- Stigler was going to have to return to his base and report that either (a) he'd failed to shoot down a helpless, limping bomber, or (b) that he'd let it go, which would likely lead to punishment.

So, weighing all of that, Stigler made a decision to do what he deemed right - follow the principle handed down by his former commanding officer - even in the face of personal cost. It certainly would have been much easier to simply shoot the bomber down and return to the accolades of his peers, but his decision speaks to the consideration of a higher ideal. Something profoundly human and brave.

In fact, when the American leaders heard the story of what

had happened, they ordered that it be kept secret because they realized that they couldn't afford to "humanize" the enemy. If pilots thought that there were other human beings in the planes they were targeting, they might think twice about doing their duty.

At your personal testing point, everything that you truly believe will be revealed. That's the essence of faith.

In your moment of testing, what will be revealed about what you truly believe? Not what you espouse because it's personally or politically beneficial to you, but the foundation of what you truly hold to be reality?

This is why the habit of immersing yourself in your vision for a better possible future is so crucial. Under pressure it's tempting to do what's convenient, but if you've spent enough time developing a sense of who you are, what you believe, and what you're working toward, the likelihood that you will do the right thing under pressure increases dramatically.

Many people spend their life living out someone else's version of who they should be - coaches, teachers, parents, peers, managers - but never spend the time necessary to refine their personal vision. Because they lack a basic framework for what a better possible future might look like, they are making decisions based upon how they feel in the moment, or based upon what others think, or because of how it might make them appear in the eyes of people they so desperately want approval from. They spend their life living someone else's narrative, and while they may succeed in achieving the approval from others that they crave, they succeed their way into failure because they lose sight of who they are and what they care about.

Yes, it is possible to succeed your way into failure.

How? By achieving everything that's valuable to others and nothing that truly matters to you. By going along with whatever cultural narrative allows you to fly under the radar and live a comfortable life while avoiding anything that personally challenges you to grow, get outside of yourself, and take chances on activities that others might disapprove of.

Here's a hard truth: others may only disapprove of your acts of bravery because your actions force them to confront their own cowardice. When you choose to step up and follow your vision, you remind them of all the ways in which they are compromising their own values and principles, which generates resentment. When they hurl critiques at you, they have one finger pointed squarely in their own chest.

So, the first step on the path to instilling a habit of bravery in your life is to become clear about what you value, why it matters to you, and how it should define your actions each and every day.

Here are the core questions that frame up your optimistic vision of a better future:

What is a primal belief that you hold, even if others think it's crazy?

What is your primary philosophy about how life works, what truly matters, and which kind of behavior is valuable in helping you align with your fundamental underlying worldview? For example, "I believe that love is the ultimate superpower" or "I believe that those who have abundance have a responsibility to aid those who are in need", or "The strong should always protect the weak", etc.

What moves you emotionally, even if others don't seem to notice?

A key indicator of our vision for a better possible future is our emotional response to the world around us. For example, are there themes within certain moments that seem to form a kind of "through-line" or pattern that point toward a deep, primal way that you are wired?

I often share with audiences I speak to about how I am profoundly moved by the stories of underdogs. Movies about people who overcame the odds and proved others around them wrong are my favorite genre. As a result, I am drawn to working with underdog companies or industries and helping them do their best, most brilliant work. In fact, when I encounter a situation in which something "extra" is required of me, it's much easier to summon the courage to act when I'm working with an organization I consider an underdog because I seem to have an extra well of energy I can tap into.

This extra well of energy is closely tied to my vision of a better possible future, in which people realize their potential regardless of their starting point. It also prompts me to step into a situation where I feel like an injustice is being committed to someone who is in a position of powerlessness. Now that I know this is a pattern, I see it everywhere in my life. It is a defining characteristic of much of my best work and many of my best moments as a human being.

So, what is that for you? When are you moved emotionally, and how might that inform your vision of a better possible future?

What are you unwilling to compromise on, no matter the cost?

Have you ever worked with someone who had an unusual behavioral pattern that you just couldn't seem to understand? For example, everything had to be returned to its proper place at the end of a meeting, or agendas were always followed to the letter, or conflict always had to be resolved in a certain way, or certain people always had to be the first to know about changes? While it may have occasionally annoyed you, you had a kind of respect for the order that it instilled in the environment. While it's possible that some of these quirks may be incidental, it's also possible that they were indicators of a deeper underlying belief or principle that these people hold and find necessary in order to pursue their vision of a better possible future.

For example, one principle that I always held deeply in a team context was to never talk about someone negatively when they weren't in the room. The net result was trust, but that wasn't why I followed it. It was just something core to my belief system.

What is that for you? What set of principles are you unwilling to compromise, regardless of the personal cost? What values do you hold dear even when it means others may look down on you or exclude you?

ACTING ON PRODUCTIVE PASSION

The belief in a better possible future doesn't imply that you have certainty about what that future holds. It's more like operating with a functioning compass than dialing up GPS directions. You know which direction you are going, but you may not be certain of how you'll get there. This is the distinction that causes many people to feel paralyzed. They exist in a state that I call "purpose paralysis". They won't move until they feel a deep certainty that they are doing the right thing.

However, this runs opposite to the manner in which nearly every brave contributor has made their mark. They didn't wait until they were certain. Rather, they had a clear sense of where they were headed, then took small steps in the direction of their vision even when they weren't sure their actions were the right ones.

As my friend Brian likes to say, "Fear is often the smell of opportunity." It's the places that we are most afraid to go that we know we most definitely should go to, but we are overcome by fear of getting it wrong.

It's likely that your compass is already pointing you toward a "magnetic North Pole", but you may not be paying attention to the clues. You suspect that you should act, but you are waiting for the GPS coordinates to kick in and the turn by turn directions to appear. They aren't coming. Instead, when you find yourself in this situation ask the following:

• What is the very next thing I could do to move me toward my vision?

• What is the immediate hurdle that I sense or am experiencing that is preventing me from acting? What can I do to mitigate its effects?

• What am I most afraid to do right now, and what might that say about what I definitely should do?

• Where am I catastrophizing or over-emphasizing the potential risks of action?

Gaining clarity about the obstacles that may be standing in your way - especially previously unconsidered ones - can help you cultivate the courage to take small steps in the direction you know you must move. However, you can't afford to wait for certainty. It's not coming.

You uncover clarity through action, not paralyzed thought. Take small steps in the direction you suspect you should go, and clarity will emerge over time like a photo in a darkroom.

ASKING BRAVE QUESTIONS

Brave people ask brave questions. The difference between a brave question and a common question is this:

A brave question is one that you don't necessarily want the answer to.

Brave questions can reveal uncomfortable truths or create accountability to act in ways you'd rather not. It might make you uncomfortable. It might require you to take a risk. It might require you to be the bigger person, or have the conversation, or share the idea, or speak truth to power. It's easier not to ask brave questions than to live with the consequences of having done so.

But here's a truth that I've experienced many times over: people are defined by the quality and courage of their questions. Those who are willing to ask brave questions often get closer to the truth faster, if they are willing to act upon what they learn.

Here are examples of brave questions:

Is this true, or do I just *want* it to be true?

If it's not true, is it possible to *make* it true?

How do I need to improve as a leader/creator/employee/ human being?

What do I suspect but am afraid to admit?

What if it *was* my fault?

What if it *wasn't* my fault?

What would I do if I wasn't afraid?

What am I willing to sacrifice in order to see it happen?

How can I make it right?

What if that's a false assumption?

Should I step up and lead?

Should I step down and let someone else take charge?

Is this confidence, or ego speaking?

Who could I ask for help?

What kind of person/leader/team member do I want to be?

It's likely that at least a few of these questions immediately resonated. Because life is often frenetic and filled with stimulus, we don't pause long enough to understand what's really on our minds - the deeper patterns, worries, suspicions, and areas of curiosity - and therefore we struggle to get to the base truths that are defining our everyday perspective of the world. When we encounter (or ask) a brave question it often jars us out of our thought rut and forces us to confront a potential truth that we'd rather not entertain.

What are your brave questions? Maybe a few are listed above, but also maybe there are others that you know you need to ask but know that doing so will force you out of your comfort zone.

Take ten minutes right now, quietly, and consider the deeper, braver questions that you've been ignoring because they might reveal an inconvenient truth. Write them down on a piece of paper or in a place where you can see them often. Taking a few minutes to consider the brave questions lurking just beneath the surface is a fantastic way to discover what's actually on your mind, and also to counter the fear-mongering narratives that prevent you from taking action on your ambitions.

Agency fuels confidence, optimism fuels progress, and

productive passion fuels optimism. As you develop your sense of agency and your vision of a better possible future, you will be positioned to act bravely when it counts. Over the next several chapters, we will apply these principles to how you work, collaborate, lead, and live.

CHECKPOINT:

Developing a clear sense of vision for the future, and cultivating optimism, is critical to your ability to develop the brave habit. Here are a few questions to consider:

1. What primal belief about the future drives you, even when others believe that you're crazy?

2. What core principles are you unwilling to compromise, even when it gets uncomfortable or costs you something?

3. Where in your life are you stalled because you lack a vision in the face of uncertainty? How could you clarify that vision?

Action Step: Think about an important decision you are facing. How can you filter that decision through your productive passion in order to gain clarity? What is your vision of a better possible future?

Be brave enough to fail your way to *growth.*

Intentions don't matter. Your *actions* define you.

CHAPTER FIVE

BRAVE WORK

"Take chances, make mistakes. That's how you grow. Pain nourishes your courage. You have to fail in order to practice being brave."

— MARY TYLER MOORE

Each and every day, you build a body of work. It consists of any place in your life where you add value, whether that's through your job, through how you lead your family, friends, or community, or even how you treat the barista at your favorite coffee shop. Your body of work stands as a testament to what you truly value, regardless of what you *say*.

Your intentions don't matter. Your actions define you.

Many people speak boldly about what they value, but their actions don't align with their words. They take arbitrary stands on issues, only to backpedal the moment that stand becomes inconvenient or gets in the way of something else they want. They are quick to judge others for not acting bravely, but they are not willing to put themselves and their reputation (or career) on the line for what they say they believe in.

You are not your work, in that it is not the sum of your identity. But in many ways, you *are* your work, because it's an expression of what you believe. Your body of work stands as a lasting testament to where you chose to spend your finite time, attention, and energy, and the impact that it has will long outlast your physical time on this planet. It will echo for years to come in the lives of the people you influence.

Are you building a body of work you can point to with pride? Is it representative of your values and aspirations, or is it the sum of your greatest compromises?

Every day, you have the precious opportunity to approach your work with an ethic of bravery. As Gretchen Rubin wrote, "What you do every day matters more than what you do once in a while." You can choose to do what's right even when it's inconvenient. You can earn the reputation of someone who backs up their words with actions. And most importantly, you have the chance to take small actions that funnel up into a body of work that represents you well.

Regardless of whether you work in the context of a team, on your own, in a workplace, remotely, and regardless of the kind of work that you do, there are principles you can follow to ensure that you are choosing brave action.

OWN YOUR WORDS AND ACTIONS

Be an individual with a backbone. If you say or do something, accept the consequences, whether good or bad, for your choices. Never throw a teammate under the bus in order to save your own reputation.

This may require a lot of bravery when the political winds are blowing against you. It's not easy to "own up" to a mistake or something you said when it means that you may have to pay a cost in order to do so. However, when you don't own your words and actions you strike a crack in your trustworthiness and weaken your foundation. You also create internal dissonance, or a gap between what you say you believe and what you actually practice. Over time, this gap can dramatically affect not only your co-workers' willingness to trust you, but even your own sense of self. It's a terrible thing when others don't trust you, but you're in a far worse state when you don't trust yourself.

It's best to own your words and actions and bravely stand behind them or admit when you are wrong. This doesn't mean playing the martyr or seeking ways to take arrows for the mistakes of others. Rather, it means a willingness to stand behind your intuition and your actions and assume responsibility for the results, whether good or bad.

Surprisingly, people trust you more when you assume responsibility for a bad result and can explain why it occurred than when you claim credit for a good result but have no idea why it was successful. Be brave enough to own what you say and what you do and your collaborators will return the favor with trust.

Question: Have you ever experienced someone refusing to own their words or actions? What did it feel like? Have you ever done it? If so, what can you do differently next time?

ENCOURAGE

This literally means to "put courage into" others. Brave people embolden the people around them, speak words of affirmation to them, and cheer them on to be their best. They are not threatened by the successes of others.

It's difficult to encourage your peers if you see the workplace as a scarce pool of resources to be fought over. It may seem like elevating the perception of a peer might be a threat to your own advancement. However, it's important to shed this scarcity mindset and recognize that there is no finite bound to available "credit". By being a person willing to speak courage into others and build their perception in the eyes of the organization (or even themselves!) you amplify generosity and goodwill among your peers. And if they don't reciprocate? Who cares! You are not responsible for their body of work, and they are not responsible for yours. The only thing you need to concern yourself with is whether you approached your work and relationships today in a manner consistent with your values.

When you're on-mission, input from others becomes an essential part of success. We need other people to help us understand ourselves fully. We can only understand who we are by fully understanding how others perceive and receive us. So, when you encourage someone else you are pouring into them a clearer sense of identity and vision for who they are when they are at their best. You help them understand how to aspire to greater impact. You infuse a vision for a better possible future, and thus cultivate an environment in which they are more poised to be brave moving forward.

If you want to work in a place where brave action is the norm, then start cultivating that environment right where you are. Own the nine square feet around you and pour courage into others when you see them doing something great.

Question: Who can you encourage today? Don't just flatter them. Be specific and pour courage into them.

EMBRACE PERSONAL GROWTH, EVEN WHEN YOU LOOK FOOLISH

Some people fear trying new things, learning new skills, or tackling new kinds of projects because they fear that if they fail they will be "found out". Brave people know that occasional failure is simply a part of doing hard things.

If you lift the same weight over and over again for five years, you will not get stronger. If you run the same distance at the same pace for months at a time, your cardiovascular health will not see much improvement. It's only when you stretch beyond your comfort zone that you begin to see results. Similarly, if you aren't learning new skills and deploying them in your work, you will eventually stagnate. If you aren't setting goals for improvement and striving to stretch yourself, your effectiveness will wane.

Be brave enough to fail your way to growth.

Don't fear failure. Fear stagnancy caused by atrophy.

Question: What do you suspect you need to get better at to help you pursue your goals, but have been avoiding?

SHARE YOUR IDEAS, EVEN WHEN THEY AREN'T RECEIVED

You cannot control whether someone else likes your ideas, but you can control whether or not you share them. The regret for inaction is too high a price to pay.

In my work with high capacity teams, one common thread among those who are especially effective is that they are quick to share ideas with one another, even before those ideas are fully formed. Doing so has a few effects:

• It sends a signal to the group that having a bad or not-fully-formed idea is often one step on the path toward having a good one.

• It shows everyone that the group is trustworthy enough to tolerate a bad idea and simply incorporate it into the process.

Sharing ideas early and often reinforces a sense of personal agency, which increases the likelihood of brave action. And, exhibiting candor in dealing with those ideas builds trust between team members as well. If an idea isn't ready for prime time, we need to acknowledge the fact and work together to improve it or find a new one. However, it's often the case that premature ideas spark insights in a teammate that lead to a more effective, mature idea. Had you never shared your initial instinct, the "a-ha!" may never have occurred.

It takes collective bravery to trust one another with our most vulnerable ideas and bits of intuition. Be brave enough to share the first idea, even when it feels risky.

Question: Is there an idea you've been holding onto that you need to share with others? When and how will you do it?

REFUSE TO COMPROMISE YOUR VALUES, EVEN WHEN IT COSTS YOU SOMETHING

Had there been more brave people willing to speak up about what they saw, fiascos like Theranos, Enron, and the Great Recession could have been averted or greatly mitigated. However, individuals often feel helpless when the problem seems so big, and realize that speaking up might cost them their reputation or career.

Brave people do what's right, even when it might cost them everything they've worked for.

If you are willing to compromise your values in small ways in order to avoid discomfort, you set yourself up to compromise in much larger, more damaging ways later. Be a person who acts upon their convictions, even when it might cost you.

What do you value and refuse to compromise on no matter what? Have you ever considered this question? If you haven't, you are more likely to be tossed with the wind, making convenient choices for personal benefit rather than acting bravely in critical moments.

Question: What are the personal values that you refuse to compromise, no matter what? Make a short list. You can refine them over time. These help define your vision of a better possible future.

COMPETE FOR PURPOSES OF CAUSE, NOT FOR COMFORT

In his book *Finite and Infinite Games*, philosopher James Carse argued that many people are often playing the wrong kind of game at the wrong time. A finite game is one where there are clear rules, a clear winner and loser, and a finite time frame. For example, football, baseball, and cricket. Everyone understands the rules and there is a clear scoreboard that determines the winner when time runs out. On the other hand, infinite games are those for which there is no end. Rather, the goal of an infinite game is to keep the game going. For example, while a CEO may say "we're going to beat the competition and be #1!", there's no such thing as "winning business." Instead, the goal is continual growth and the pursuit of results that matter to the organization, whatever they might be.

As you consider your work and your career, are you approaching it with a finite, or an infinite mindset? Are you simply competing against others in order to get the next promotion, or is there something else you are pursuing that transcends the temporary wins and losses you experience along the way? Cowards climb the ladder because of what it brings them in terms of comfort and accolades. Brave people are driven by principles and cause.

To be clear, there is nothing wrong with comfort as a by-product of great work. Comfort is not the enemy. The pursuit of comfort in the place of the pursuit of great work causes many people to settle into a place of mediocrity and cowardice. If comfort is more important to you than cause, you are more likely to make choices that feel good but take you nowhere.

Increased platform equals increased impact, but to what end? If climbing the ladder is solely for purposes of "winning" a finite game inside of your organization, your success will eventually feel hollow. However, if you see your career progress as a means to increase your impact and influence on those around you, you are playing an infinite game where everyone wins when you succeed. Be the person who bravely competes on the basis of cause, not comfort.

Question: What is the infinite game you are playing? What greater cause or good are you pursuing?

Your work is an expression of what you value. How you collaborate, lead, and add value to the people around you funnels up into a body of work that will stand as a testament to your time on this planet.

Will that body of work represent you well?

The best way to minimize regret is to work bravely.

CHECKPOINT:

Every day you build a body of work that stands as a testament to your time on earth. Consider the following:

1. Do you tend to take ownership of your words and actions, or do you cast blame? How can you better own the outcomes of your work?

2. Who can you put courage into this today? This week?

3. What new skill do you need to develop, even if you might look incompetent for a season?

4. What are the personal values that drive your decisions? Write them out and keep them in front of you consistently throughout the week.

Action Step: Consider one brave action that you need to take in your work this week. When will you act?

Brave
people
embolden
others.

Commit to going *first.*

CHAPTER SIX

BRAVE TEAMS

"When spiders unite, they can tie down a lion."

— ETHIOPIAN PROVERB

Most of us do our work in the context of others. We depend on teammates to provide perspective or skills that we don't have, and they likewise rely on us to deliver our part. When trust is high and competence is apparent, teams can function like well-oiled machines. However, when either breaks down it can begin a downward spiral, a "doom loop" in the words of Jim Collins, that threatens to stall the entire organization.

When a perception exists that *some* members of the team are willing to engage in brave action while others tend to retreat from discomfort, it generates uncertainty and doubt that leads to hesitation when action is needed. On the other hand, when brave action becomes the expected norm, and that expectation is reinforced by both stated metrics and the rewards structure of the organization, the entire team benefits. This is what we could call "conspicuous courage".

Brave action tends to lead to more brave action. When you act bravely, you give me permission to do the same.

I see this all the time in companies I work with. When I ask an uncomfortable question of a leadership team, for example "what's something you're doing right now that needs to stop, even if it's difficult to do so?", I'm met with silence. People look around the room or look down at their notebook to avoid eye contact. Then, one person sheepishly raises their hand and shares a hesitant answer. "Well, I know it's in the best interest of our clients, but we keep making promises that my team is unaware of, then we are surprised and often challenged to deliver on them by the time we find out."

A conversation ensues, and the head of accounts agrees that there needs to be better communication before making promises to clients, even if it causes delays. Then another response to the question. And another. So many issues that were previously unaddressed, though deeply affecting the team.

What brought them into the light? A direct question followed by one brave person willing to go first.

Are *you* willing to go first? Are you willing to commit to a culture of vulnerability and empathy even at the risk of it not being reciprocated? Are you willing to share the first response even when it might cause conflict with others?

To cultivate an environment of bravery, commit to going *first*. This means taking agency in the midst of uncertainty, and acting with your vision of a better possible future firmly in mind. If each team member commits to acting with Perceived Agency and Optimistic Vision, you'll create a fertile field for strategic risk-taking and collaborative trust.

ENGAGE IN (HEALTHY) CONFLICT

I often hear managers say something to the effect of "We're about the healthiest team you'll ever meet - we never fight!" (I want to reply "You are profoundly dysfunctional!" but what I *actually* say is "Tell me more.") Healthy teams fight. However, they do it in healthy ways. Conflict is the natural result of talented, motivated people bumping into one another. If your organization has hired well, you will naturally find yourself in situations where the strong and viable opinions of team members run in opposition to one another. That's fine, and expected. However, the way in which you handle that conflict is everything.

Brave teams are willing to wade into conflict and have difficult conversations before those disagreements create fissures in the culture. When disagreements are left untended for too long, they forge an undertow in team meetings, pulling everyone back under the water no matter how hard they fight to escape. If you don't want to be having the same conversation in a different form three months from now, be candid and urgent about addressing conflict.

Be honest about disagreements. Don't pretend that everyone is on the same page if you're not. Share perspectives openly, and voice your opinion in a respectful way. There's another name for false harmony: dysfunction. All of those bad feelings are just being pushed beneath the surface where they are likely to re-emerge at a later, and maybe less opportune, time. Cultivate an environment in which disagreement is celebrated as a sign of thought-sharpening rather than a sign of someone just being difficult.

Recognize authority. Just because you are given permission to speak doesn't mean you have authority to make the decision. It takes bravery to share your thoughts knowing that it may not do much to move the needle. Do it anyway. It makes the team stronger. Plus, it's likely that others on the team are thinking the same thing and your willingness to speak up may help them choose brave action next time as well.

Never, ever let it get personal. Make certain that your disagreements about ideas don't become personality cults. The moment conflict becomes personal, everyone loses. Do your best to ensure that conflict is handled in the open, and on a professional level. Brave teams keep it about the work, and are willing to curb their deeper insecurities and the instinct to fight for turf.

Brave teams fight well. Cowardly teams run from conflict. Healthy conflict builds better work and better teams.

Question: Is there any place where you are avoiding conflict, or trying to pre-maturely squash it in order to avoid discomfort? What would it look like to address the situation head-on with empathy and bravery?

PROTECT YOUR TEAMMATES

Brave teammates stand up for and protect their fellow teammates' reputations. When someone else is speaking ill of their teammate, they don't join in. They recognize that trust is earned every single day, and that it's often not the big violations that cause trust to be broken but the small ones. Trust must be fought for and preserved. Some lines cannot be crossed.

On the other hand, cowards throw people under the bus in order to save their own skin. They are willing to allow someone else to take arrows - rightly or wrongly - in order to preserve their own reputation. Their vision of a better possible future is primarily driven by their own self-interest, not that of their collective team and stakeholders.

This only sounds naive to those whose primary lens of the world is pessimistic. When your core belief system is centered on preserving and protecting what's "yours" because you believe there are a finite amount of resources and opportunity, your instinct is to lash out and defend yourself at all costs or to relish seeing someone else losing something that you believe you deserve. However, when your primary story is one of optimism - that there are ample opportunities for those who are willing to do the work and seize the moment - you feel less resentment toward those who have what you feel you deserve.

But this isn't just "feel good" advice. It's also very, very practical. You want others rooting for you when you have an important opportunity. You need their support when you take a risk. You have to be able to trust them when they give you advice. If those bonds have been frayed because you've been quietly rooting against them, or if you view everyone around you suspiciously because of your fundamental belief in a "zero sum" game, you will be less likely to depend on the perspective of others and thus more likely to make avoidable mistakes. You will reap later what you invest today. Being a trust-worthy teammate now yields much needed goodwill later.

Question: Has someone ever blamed you for something in order to protect their own reputation? How did it feel? How might you have acted differently in their situation?

RECOGNIZE THAT IT'S NOT ABOUT YOU

Brave teammates know that the cause supersedes any individual credit they receive. It's not about their idea, it's about the right idea. They are willing to support the best work, even if it's at the expense of personal recognition.

Just like other advice in this section, it's important not only because it's the right thing to do, but because next time it may be your idea that's on the table and you want others to support you. If you are willing to throw your support behind an idea that you believe to be best even though it means forfeiting your own piece of credit, you invest in tremendous goodwill that is likely to return to you later.

Bravery is about making investments now that may not pay dividends in the immediate term, but that you believe will pay off huge in the long run. It's doing the right thing now even when you can't see immediate results, but trusting that results will follow. This is essential in relationships, and even more so in highly interdependent, collaborative ones.

Question: What investments could you make in other people today? How might you encourage and elevate others in order to cultivate an environment in which brave action is more likely?

BRAVELY GIVE AND RECEIVE FEEDBACK

Brave teammates are willing to hear feedback they disagree with and are not afraid to offer helpful feedback when they believe a fellow teammate is not living up to their potential. No one wins when we hide the truth in order to be liked. This is putting yourself ahead of the productive passion of the team. Instead, be willing to risk being unliked for a season if it means helping others become better and achieve their desired results.

Now, this isn't permission to be abusive or rude. Feedback should be delivered in a manner that can be received by the other person. However, candor is a critical quality of high functioning teams. Teams who trust one another enough to speak directly and bravely never question what the other person on the team *really* thinks. They know that nothing is being strategically hidden in order to avoid discomfort.

Question: Is there any feedback that you need to give someone else, but have been avoiding? When will you have the conversation?

We rise and fall together. One act of cowardice on a team can shape the team's perception of what's possible and what's not. However, one act of bravery grants permission to others to take strategic risk, have difficult conversations, offer edgy ideas, and commit to deliverables that feel a little out of reach. This is how we grow.

While a forest may seem from the outside observer like a random collection of individual trees and plants, scientists have recently come to discover that it is actually, in many ways, a single, complex organism. Trees and plants communicate with one another through an interconnected web of roots and microbes, sharing both information and resources when necessary.

While much of the communication is designed to help same-species plants survive and reproduce, there is evidence that cross-species cooperation also occurs with the purpose of keeping the forest ecosystem alive and viable. An article [1] on the Harvard University Graduate School Of Arts and Sciences website shared how some of these mechanisms function.

"Similarly, there is cross-talk between different species of

---

[1] *Exploring The Underground Network of Trees*, Harvard.edu

trees that share the same mycorrhizal network, such as between birch and fir trees. Interspecies tree communication has been shown to increase the fitness and resiliency of trees." The article continues, "Mycorrhizal networks are extremely important for tree health during times of danger. Certain species of fungi can facilitate tree resilience to certain environmental stressors such as predators, toxins, and pathogenic microbes that invade an ecosystem. By using a technique called allelopathy, in which a chemical signal is sent through the mycorrhizal network, trees can warn their neighbors about an invasive predator or to inhibit growth of invasive plant species. Surrounding trees can then defend themselves by releasing volatile hormones or chemicals to deter predators or pathogenic bugs. It was even found that trees can send a stress signal to nearby trees after a major forest disturbance, such as deforestation."

While every tree is certainly behaving in such a way to ensure its own survival and that of its species, there is a biological reality that a diverse, thriving ecosystem in which everyone prospers is best for long-term resilience.

The same principle applies to your team. The best way for you to ensure your own long-term viability is to act bravely, share generously, engage with empathy, speak directly, and raise the expectations for the entire ecosystem to do the same.

Be a brave teammate. Go first.

CHECKPOINT:

You do your work in the company of others. Consider the following:

1. Is there any unresolved conflict that you need to bravely address?

2. Do you have a teammate that you need to commit to protecting, even when it gets uncomfortable?

3. What feedback have you been holding onto because you've been afraid to share it?

4. What does it mean for you to deliver that feedback in an empathetic way?

Action Step: Consider one brave action that you need to take with your peers this week. When will you act?

Brave action leads to *more* brave action.

Brave leaders communicate *clearly* in the midst of uncertainty.

CHAPTER SEVEN

BRAVE LEADERS

"Courage is what it takes to stand up and speak;
courage is also what it takes to sit down and listen."

— **WINSTON S. CHURCHILL**

As a leader, you may think that your job is to get the work done. It's not.

Your job is to create an environment in which *others* can get the work done. Your job isn't to do the work, it's to *lead* the work. These are fundamentally different responsibilities.

And, a primary function of that responsibility is cultivating an environment that is conducive to brave action. This means that you consistently (a) fuel and refine a vision of a better possible future, and (b) speak agency into those who are responsible for helping bring it about.

Agency and Optimism are the twin engines of innovative teams, and you control the throttle. However, simply piling on platitudes or flattering team members won't get you very far.

Your leadership should be infused with authenticity, be precise, and prove to others that you are willing to put just as much skin in the game as they are being asked to do.

Bravado is talking a big game while keeping a safe distance. Bravery is putting yourself on the line for the results. It means that you are willing to cast a big vision, fight for the resources needed to accomplish that vision, and align yourself with the team, whatever the results.

BE CAREFUL WHAT YOU WISH FOR

But, do you really want brave work? Before you instinctively respond "yes!", understand the implications of what you're asking for. Brave work means conflict, because team members will have different understandings of risk. It also means failure in both big and small ways. It means difficult conversations, accountability, emotional volatility, anxiety, and risk of reputation. It also means that you will need to fight for your team's space to do its brave work. You will have to defend the needed resources. And, you will have to take arrows from others who don't understand what you're trying to do.

If we're being honest, many leaders and organizations don't want employees making brave decisions. Bravery equals risk, which equals potential disequilibrium, which leads to potential failure and blame. Brave action means culpability if things go awry. Instead, we prefer the comfortable confines of what Stanford professor Steve Blank calls "innovation theater".

In an article for *Harvard Business Review*[1], Blank argued that many organizations strive for the appearance of risk-taking and innovation while simultaneously protecting the organization from any real or disruptive change. He wrote "Companies and government agencies typically adopt innovation activities (hackathons, design thinking classes, innovation workshops, et al.) that result in innovation theater. These activities shape and build culture, but they don't win wars, and they rarely deliver shippable/deployable product." This creates the appearance of brave action without the requisite risk. The trouble with this approach is that most employees can see through the ploy and find this kind of faux bravery dispiriting and demotivating. Truly talented people don't want to work in a place where their best efforts are spent just holding the place together.

This is why a culture of bravery begins with leaders choosing to make brave action a habit. They model the way for the rest of the organization, put on full display the difference between bold action and true bravery, demonstrate the nuances of calculated vs. stupid risk, and reward behavior that might be uncomfortable but that reinforces the desired culture of the organization.

In *Herding Tigers* I wrote about the importance of leaders monitoring not just the organizational scoreboard, or the metrics by which they determine the successful output of the team, but also the organizational dashboard, which are the leading indicators of team health. One of the most important dashboard

---

[1] *Why Companies Do "Innovation Theater" Instead of Actual Innovation*, HBR.org

items for leaders of talented, creative people is the presence of brave action in the workplace. Here are a few places to look for it:

Are people sharing ideas freely, or only rallying around safe ones? When the potential consequences of sharing an outlier idea outweigh the potential benefits of success, people gravitate toward safety over contribution. Are team members introducing ideas that turn your head?

Is conflict being handled directly and well? Conflict is the natural result of talented, creative people bumping into one another. If you've hired well, and the people on your team are driven to do great work, they will inevitably disagree. However, with regard to the health of the team, how conflict is handled is everything. Are team members resolving their disagreements, or simply ignoring them and allowing them to fester? It takes brave action to work out conflict directly and swiftly, with empathy.

Are individuals taking accountability, or are project leaders deflecting responsibility to the team? When a culture of comfort and fear takes root, teams tend toward group decision-making and consensus rather than holding individuals responsible for results. A culture of brave action is a culture of accountability, where the stakes are clear and ownership is defined.

This is not a game for the faint of heart. True leadership - brave leadership - is not something to be trifled with. If you're not committed, it's better to let someone else take the helm.

More damage is done by half-committed leaders than those who never commit.

But, if you are willing to step up for your team and cultivate an environment of brave action, the rewards are infinite.

Again, in order to do so you will need to facilitate an environment of optimistic vision and agency.

CULTIVATING OPTIMISTIC VISION

The chief enemy of optimism is uncertainty. The work that you and your team do is complex, and with that complexity comes an almost endless string of possibilities. How do you know which decision to make? How do you know which approach will deliver the most value for your stakeholders?

Here's where the role of the leader becomes critical: In the face of uncertainty, it's tempting to become *imprecise*. You waffle. You offer vague direction instead of clear-headed encouragement. By doing this, you allow a lack of clarity to take root within the team's culture, because clarity requires commitment. To say yes to one option, you must say no to many others. As this lack of clarity becomes more dominant, a vacuum emerges that is often filled with a dozen different narratives about where the team is headed, why decisions are being made the way they are, and who is ultimately responsible for what.

Lack of clarity is the mortal enemy of optimistic vision.

If your team members are constantly negotiating between conflicting stories of why their work matters, they will struggle to do any work that challenges the status quo. In order to cultivate an environment of brave action, a vision of a better possible future must be crystal clear, communicated regularly, and deeply connected to everyday work. If you want others to take risks with their work, you must take the first risk by committing to a vision.

This doesn't mean that the vision can't evolve over time as you learn and grow. Of course it will. But, it's important that at any given point in time your team knows precisely where it is headed, why it matters, and what is required of them in order to get there.

If you want people to spend themselves on behalf of a cause, you'd better ensure that the cause is clearly understood and embraced.

CULTIVATING AGENCY

In complex workplaces, it's often difficult to feel the connection between the work that you do each day and the end product. Layers of meetings, complex conversations, iterations and adaptations, and suddenly "Voila! C'est fini!" But, you were just one cog in a whirling machine.

Over time, this can lead to a sense of disconnect between actions and results. While you have no doubt that you are adding value to the process, it can feel like nothing is really *yours*. There is no sense of ownership of the final product because ownership is spread quite thin. Of course, when you lack a sense of ownership of the work, your connection to why that work matters becomes even more obscured.

Therefore, as a leader it is essential that you help the members of your team understand the direct connection between the work that they do each day and the ultimate why of that work. Not in the grand, existential, "why am I here on this planet?" sense, but in the very practical "why does your effort and sacrifice on this project help us move toward our objectives?" People need to feel like they aren't just spinning plates, but are making a direct contribution to the cause. More importantly, they need to understand how their unique skill set is targeted at that cause. They need to see the connection between their actions and the ultimate results. When they can't see that connection, dissonance emerges. Dissonance is the gap between the "what" and the "why" of work, and it causes many workers to feel a deep disconnect from the team and its ambitions.

Dissonance is the mortal enemy of agency.

When it feels like nothing you do ultimately matters that much, it can feel like you are simply a victim of the organizational currents. While you may work hard each day, you ultimately feel like you lack any influence over the direction of the work or its impact.

As the leader, you can help your team members reclaim their sense of agency by routinely reinforcing (a) their unique role in the work and your expectations of their contribution, and (b) the connection between their efforts and the ultimate results of the team's work.

The greatest tool you have in your battle against dissonance is simplicity. The more simply and directly you can connect the team's actions to the results, the greater the sense of agency they will feel and the more likely they are to do brave work. Removing unnecessary complexity, offering simple and direct communication and expectations, and consistently drawing a connection between the work we are doing today and the results we will see tomorrow are core elements of cultivating an environment of Perceived Agency.

BRAVE LEADERSHIP IN PRACTICE

Brave workplaces need brave leaders. They need people who are committed to standing in the gap, protecting their people, and fighting for the mission of the organization even at personal expense. However, all of the talk and bluster in the world will not produce results.

People won't believe what you say until you earn trust through what you *do*.

Here are a few core practices that brave leaders can implement in order to cultivate an environment of brave action:

Have the uncomfortable conversation

It's tempting to avoid conversations that are (a) inconvenient because they use time that could be spent doing work, or (b) will generate conflict because they are about a volatile topic like performance, or attitude. It's far easier to avoid such difficult chats with direct reports and simply go about your work as if nothing is wrong, hoping they'll resolve on their own. However, those situations typically don't magically resolve, and the net result is decreased stability in your team's culture. If your team sees that you are unwilling to take uncomfortable steps to address behavior that's inconsistent with what you say you value, you will lose their trust in other areas that really matter, such as believing you'll have their back if they take a risk and fail.

To be clear, this doesn't mean that you should seek conflict or be a total jerk whenever you see something you dislike. Use discernment about when to engage in these difficult conversations. Identify a few key principles that you are going to address every time, and recognize that some things may have to slip in the interim. But, you can't afford to allow destructive behavior or misaligned activity that could cause problems later. When you fail to intervene, your team begins to question whether you'll exhibit bravery elsewhere and it will affect their willingness to follow you.

Brave leaders recognize that it's more important to be effective than to be liked. This doesn't mean that you can't be both liked and effective - of course you can - but you cannot prioritize both in equal measure. In order to inspire a culture of brave action, it's more important that you be trusted than liked. This means having difficult conversations with your team in a respectful and timely manner.

Question: Are there any difficult conversations you've been avoiding? How might this be affecting your team's clarity about what you truly value, or their willingness to trust you when things get difficult?

Speak truth to power

You cannot afford to be two-faced, saying one thing to your team and another to your leadership. Because leadership is ultimately about being in the middle - leading both up and down - some leaders succumb to the pressure to complain about the organization to their team while complaining about their team to the organization.

Brave leaders are willing to fight for principles even at the risk of being ground in the organizational gears. They are consistent in their perspective in every conversation and environment. While it's wise to be ever-mindful of the political winds, they don't play political games. Rather, they understand that their primary responsibility is to equip the team they lead to help the organization accomplish its mission.

Are you willing to disagree with your manager or with the leaders of your organization, or do you hide inconvenient truths in order to avoid difficult conversations?

Do you reveal difficult truths about priorities and resources with your manager, or do you just placate your team by grumbling about "they or them" when you don't get what you need?

Do you respectfully challenge your manager or leadership when they act inconsistently with your organization's stated mission or culture?

Do you demand the same respect for your team from the organization as the organization demands from them?

Question: What is something you know you need to talk about with your manager, but have been avoiding because it will be uncomfortable or could result in conflict?

Put your resources where your mouth is

Cowardly leaders say bold things, but are always hedging their bets. They love to proclaim all of the things they will do someday, but always seem to have an excuse at the ready for why they aren't taking action. Or worse, they pile work on their team without any understanding of what it will actually take to accomplish that work. They allow their team to take the hit for the unrealistic expectations of the organization.

Brave leaders are willing to put themselves on the line by resourcing the initiatives they believe to be best for the organization and the people it serves. They don't ask their team to do something that they're not willing to (a) resource fully and (b) protect their space to produce. Many leaders lose their team's trust by continually piling more work on top of an already overflowing stack - just one more thing - without any accommodation for how that work will get done. Often, this is because someone in the organization has asked for unrealistic results, and rather than have the difficult conversation and setting realistic expectations, they simply push the pressure down to their team. This is cowardice, because it's protecting yourself at the expense of those you are supposed to protect.

When was the last time you had a direct conversation about whether your team has the time and attention needed to do the work you're asking of them? Do you ever push back on requests from your organization or try to find a more reasonable way for your team to tackle its work?

If your team is so inundated with work that it's fighting to keep its head above water, innovative, brave work will be non-existent in your culture. Bravery requires opportunity and resources, and if your team is struggling to meet its baseline expectations, it's unlikely that anyone will pause to consider new, better, more innovative ways to approach a project.

Question: Is there any work that your team is doing that is under-resourced? Have a conversation with your team members about what they need in order to do the work you've asked of them.

Give your job away

Insecure leaders fear that someone will take their place. They hoard information, protect their contacts and relationships, and always need to be the "bridge" between two people in order to ensure that they are seen as valuable to the organization. They are paranoid. Their biggest phobia is being seen as irrelevant.

Brave leaders are secure. They recognize that their job is to reproduce themselves in others around them and to train other people up to shoulder organizational responsibility. They know that the greatest mark of leadership is when they have made themselves irrelevant by reproducing other team members who could easily step in and lead in their place.

How often do you speak courage and agency into others and give them the opportunity to stretch their responsibilities? Do you empower people on your team to make decisions, or do you need to be directly involved in every decision in order to ensure that nothing goes awry?

Do you lead by principle or by presence? Said differently, do you teach others *how* to make decisions and *why* those decisions work, then trust them to act as independent agents? Or, do you need to be physically present for each decision in order to trust that the work will meet your standards?

Your measure of effectiveness as a leader is how much you grow the team's capacity to do brilliant work in your absence. If you hoard information, protect decision-making power, and dominate the process, then your team's capacity will never expand beyond your personal purview. However, if you empower your team, listen to them, teach them how you make decisions and the principles behind them, and give responsibility away, your team's capacity will know no limits.

Question: Are you protecting your role, or giving it away? Are you focused on developing other leaders, or on enacting your will through other people?

Brave cultures rest on the shoulders of brave leaders. Speak agency into your team members. Tell them what they are capable of, even if they don't see it yet. Help them make direct connections between their everyday work and the better future you are pursuing together. Be clear even when you are uncertain. Eliminate pointless complexity, and fight for the resources your team requires.

Be the brave leader your team needs.

CHECKPOINT:

Your team needs you to model brave action. Consider the following:

1. Is there an uncomfortable conversation that you've been avoiding? When will you have it?

2. Have you painted a clear vision of the future for your team? Have they been equipped with the belief that they can help bring it about?

3. Is there any "truth" that you need to speak to your manager or organization, but have been afraid to do so?

4. Where do you hold onto your role or responsibility in a way that limits your team's effectiveness? How can you release some control?

Action Step: Consider one brave action that you need to take in your leadership this week. When will you act?

Brave leaders
eliminate
pointless
complexity.

Brave people protect those who can't protect themselves.

Cowards *exploit*.

CHAPTER EIGHT

BRAVE NEIGHBORS

"We are all in the same boat, in a stormy sea, and we owe each other a terrible loyalty."

— G.K. CHESTERTON

While much of this book has been targeted at brave action in the workplace, we also need to address the importance of brave action in the places where we live. Great nations and municipalities are sustained by great neighborhoods, and great neighborhoods are forged by brave neighbors.

I'll fully admit that it's possible that my perspective on this subject is skewed by endless hours spent in front of the TV as a youth watching a Pittsburgh Presbyterian pastor extol the responsibilities and wonders of community. Fred Rogers launched the TV show *Mr. Rogers' Neighborhood* in 1968 with the goal of reclaiming the medium of television and bringing a sense of stability, encouragement, and community to children in his city, and soon beyond. The show ran for thirty-one seasons and spanned four decades, impacting the lives of millions of children. Most adults between the ages of twenty-five and sixty-five instinctively complete the musical phrase, "would you be mine, could you be mine..." with "...won't you be my neighbor?" In a 2018 documentary about Rogers' life called *Won't You Be My Neighbor*, he expands on his philosophy:

"Love is at the root of everything - all learning, all parenting, all relationships. Love or the lack of it. And what we see and hear on the screen is part of who we become."

Rogers believed that children needed to see models of generosity, kindness, healthy conflict resolution, dealing with anger and frustration, and citizenship. Through the recurring characters and rhythmic rituals of his episodes, he aimed to provide a stable, safe environment for children to learn about the world, including its more uncomfortable realities. Rogers directly dealt with issues such as racism, death, divorce, and social class in his programs, teaching children to engage with one another with empathy and directness.

If Rogers' philosophy "what we see and hear on the screen is part of who we become" is to be believed, blame for the significant downward spiral in civility and empathy in our culture could be largely placed on the shoulders of our leaders and media influencers. It's rare to find examples of cooperation, collaborative problem-solving, self-sacrifice, and - in the words of Rogers - love modeled through today's media. Many if not most people have grown jaded and skeptical of the agenda-driven "news" from each side of the political spectrum (or worse, only from the side they disagree with) while we have felt simultaneously de-humanized by a media who wants to split us easily divisible segments in order to sell us soap, pills, and pillows.

If change is going to happen for the better, it will begin in our neighborhoods. We can commit to engaging bravely with one another, protecting one another, and forming alliances that help us stand for common values. We can re-humanize, re-connect, and engage in brave conversations with others who may (gasp!) disagree with our perspective. Doing so doesn't mean we have to end in agreement, but only that we are able to find common ground in the larger principles that bind us together.

HOW TO BE A BRAVE NEIGHBOR

Let me be clear and say that I'm not pointing fingers at you. No, this is also a finger in my own chest. It's a call to action for all of us to act bravely within the space where we have the most direct influence: our homes, and our neighborhoods.

Here are a few principles for being a brave neighbor:

Build real relationships with people who don't look or think like you

It's natural to gravitate toward relationships that make us feel comfortable. This means that we prefer to be around people who have the same interests, perhaps the same income level, and same political opinions. There's nothing wrong with this. It's a part of what allowed humans to survive and flourish in times when being excluded from a tribe meant being abandoned to the elements and almost certain death. Having commonality within your group meant your identity and protection was secured.

However, in today's world these natural herding instincts that protected us in a world of warring tribes is betraying us. Isolation and dehumanization lead to cultural death in a hyper-connected world where societies thrive through understanding and collaboration more than dominance.

Brave neighbors take bold steps toward inclusion, and are willing to invite others into their comfortable circles. They seek commonality. They initiate conversations.

Recently, I heard Cynt Marshall, CEO of the Dallas Mavericks basketball team, speak at an event about the importance of inclusion in the business world. She said, "Diversity is being invited to the party. Inclusion is being asked to dance."

Be the neighbor who invites others to dance.

Question: Do you seek out relationships with people in your sphere of influence who don't necessarily think or look like you?

Protect one another

Brave neighbors watch out for one another and are willing to step in and intervene when there is an injustice or cowardly action affecting their neighbor.

Once I was scheduled to speak at an event in New York City

at the very end of a long string of speaking engagements. I was tired from my travels, but fortunately, my hotel was only a few blocks from the venue so I decided that a nice mid-morning stroll down the streets of the city would be a great way to spark my mind awake and get me in the mood for my talk. About halfway to the venue, I noticed a commotion at the side of the street. A man was yelling at a woman, who was crying and screaming at him. Around them a few dozen people had gathered, many of them holding their phones up to record the interaction. I made my way closer to the altercation, and quickly realized that this was a dispute over cab fare. The cab driver had taken hold of the woman's purse and was shaking it back and forth as the woman refused to let go.

In that moment, something welled up inside of me. To be honest, I didn't know who was right or wrong in the situation - maybe the woman was trying to stiff the cabbie - but regardless, there was no excuse for a man twice her size to be exerting that kind of physical force and intimidation on her. I stepped through the cell phone gawkers and injected myself into the situation.

"What's going on?" I asked.

"She owes me money for her fare," the cab driver replied.

"I don't owe anything!" the woman replied, "And, he's making me late for my job interview. I need this job." Her face was red, and her makeup was beginning to run down her face because of the tears. She was obviously shaken.

I looked straight into the cab driver's eyes and said as firmly as I could muster "Let it go." He could tell that I meant business. A woman who had previously been watching from the sidelines came over and I asked her if she could help the crying woman. They walked over to the curb to search for the building where her job interview was scheduled.

Once I knew the crying woman was alright, I diverted my attention back to the cab driver. "OK," I said. "I'm going to make this right with you. But before I do, I need you to promise me something. You can never, ever do that to a woman again. Do you understand how frightening it is to someone for a big, aggressive man to be tugging at her purse?"

He said he understood, and although he initially tried to justify what he did, he eventually apologized for his actions.

"How much do you believe she owes you?" I asked, prepared to part with fifty dollars or more.

"Five dollars."

I was stunned. All of this for five bucks. This whole spectacle was over what amounted to an overpriced latte.

I pulled out my wallet and handed him a ten, which was the smallest bill that I had.

"You promise me you will never do this again?" I asked before I let go of the bill.

"I promise."

He got back in the cab, and I continued on to the venue. The cell phone gawkers resumed their day. My mind was certainly sparked.

I tell this story not in order to say "Hey! Look at this thing I did!" but to prod you to consider that you've probably done the *exact same thing* at some point in your life. Maybe you didn't intervene in an altercation, but there was some circumstance that compelled action and before you knew it you were squarely in the middle of the action. These moments punctuate our lives, but we often discount them and just move on with our responsibilities.

While moments like this don't happen every day, there are ways in which we can seek to protect our neighbors in less obvious but probably more important ways. For example, walking an older neighbor home or helping them with their groceries. Checking in on a single parent to see if they need any help. Keeping a watch over the neighborhood kids and sharing with their parents when you see them doing something incredibly amazing or frighteningly dangerous.

We need others to stand in the gap and protect us, and they need us to do the same for them.

Question: What would it look like for you to become a protector in your neighborhood?

Do the unseen things

Brave neighborhoods are forged by people who do the right thing, even when it's never seen by their neighbors. They try to make the world around them a little better than they found it. And, they don't need credit for what they do. They do it because it's the right thing.

One of the many things I greatly admire about my wife is her commitment to the principle of doing the unseen things. We routinely take long evening walks around our neighborhood, and on one of them we came across some litter at an intersection and she remarked "ugh - I can't believe people just throw their trash out on the side of the road." While most people would have just waited for the street cleaners to take care of it, the next day she brought a trash bag with her in order to collect the garbage we encountered along our walk. Did she do it for the credit? Of course not. She did it because it made our neighborhood a little better. Even if no one noticed, she would know.

What small, unseen behaviors would make your neighborhood a better place to live? How might you show love to those around you by doing what everyone else thinks of but doesn't actually *do*? By engaging in these kinds of behaviors, you model agency for everyone around you and you paint a picture of a better possible future. In other words, you forge an environment in which brave action is more likely to occur. Serve one another, even when your actions are invisible to those around you.

Question: What "unseen" actions might you commit to as an act of service to your neighborhood?

Listen, I know that this chapter might feel a little out of place in a book where we've been talking about launching ideas and collaborating on projects. However, you cannot separate your work life from every other part of your experience. You are at the

126

center of every commitment you make, and therefore every experience you have is an opportunity to develop the habit of bravery or succumb to the comfort of cowardice. When you choose brave action in your neighborhood you are preparing yourself for your next big presentation, and when you have a difficult conversation with your boss you are reinforcing the habits you will need to forge friendships with people you disagree with.

We need brave leaders willing to do what's right in the face of discomfort right in the place where they live. Will that be you?

Or in the words of the immortal philosopher, "won't you be my neighbor?"

CHECKPOINT:

Great communities are built upon great neighborhoods. Consider the following:

1. How can you be more intentional about the relationships in your neighborhood?

2. What does it look like to be a "protector" in your neighborhood?

3. What small actions can you take to improve where you live?

Action Step: Consider one brave action that you need to take in your neighborhood this week. When will you act?

Your name is whatever you choose to *answer* to.

CHAPTER NINE

BRAVE NEW WORLD

"Ultimately, man should not ask what the meaning of his life is, but rather must recognize that it is he who is asked. In a word, each man is questioned by life; and he can only answer to life by answering for his own life; to life he can only respond by being responsible."

—VIKTOR FRANKL, MAN'S SEARCH FOR MEANING

Several years ago my family went camping in a place called Mammoth Cave, in Kentucky. As part of the trip my wife informed me (as often happens in our household) that we were going to be making a little side excursion to a place called Horse Cave where, as she put it, we would engage in "a little light rappelling". The reason my wife had to warn me in advance about this little rappelling adventure is that she knows that since well before we were married I have been afraid of heights. But, she consoled me, it's probably a very short cliff. After all, even our kids who were much younger at the time were able to rappel, so how bad could it be? And, she added, it ends in a pizza buffet. (If you want to get me onboard with any plan, just tell me it ends at a pizza buffet.)

The time came for us to make our little side excursion, and as we were "gearing up" to rappel I remember thinking "wow - this is a lot of gear we're wearing for a little 'kid cliff'." We had helmets, and pads, and the kind of harnesses you normally see daredevils and soldiers wearing. I started to get nervous as I glanced around at the twenty-five or so heavily armored people in our group.

Then, I received two pieces of information I did not previously have. The first was that it wasn't, in fact, a little "kid cliff", but was instead a sheer 80 foot cliff that emptied out into another 120 foot drop into Horse Cave. I got a little tense. However, the second piece of information held my salvation in its grasp. Our guide informed us that there was now a lightning storm headed into the area, and if the lightning storm came in quicker than expected there was a good chance that not everyone would be able to go over the cliff.

As you can imagine, I developed a new strategy. I was going to be the most polite rappeller in the history of Horse Cave. As we made our way out to the cliff, I was letting every single person in our party ahead of me. "No, you go first. Please! I *really* want this experience, but I want it for you *more*." As we arrived out to the cliff, I was the very last person in line out of approximately twenty-five people in our group. I was singing praises to my own brilliance! I thought I'd managed to successfully escape having to rappel while simultaneously looking like a really good guy.

Then, I looked up. At the very front of the line was my nine-year-old daughter Ava. Her eyes were filled with excitement and she couldn't *wait* to go over the cliff. Almost as if he was taunting me, our guide put his hand on Ava's helmet and proclaimed "Look at this brave young lady! How daring and fearless is she to be willing to be first over the cliff?!? Is there any mere mortal as courageous as she?" (OK, I may have made that last part up.) "But," he added, "we can't have a child go first. We need an adult to go first."

Ava immediately turned and looked right at me.

At that moment a switch flipped in me. I've spent a lot of time in the years since this happened trying to understand what changed, and I believe I've arrived at an answer, which I'll share in a moment. Almost as if having an out of body experience, I immediately raised my hand, and said "I'll go," adding under my breath "I want to die *quickly* and with *honor*."

I walked over to the "precipice of death" and our guide hooked me in and told me to lean back over the cliff. I felt the line grow taught, and as I began down the rock wall I realized that the mechanism was actually holding my weight. In fact, I was enjoying myself. As I got about fifteen feet down, almost out of earshot, I heard the guide suddenly proclaim "OK, folks. Apparently the lightning storm is coming in quicker than we

131

thought…"

For a moment, it was as if I was the butt of a giant cosmic joke.

However, his point was that we would need to hurry to get everyone over the cliff, which we did and it was a great experience. And, might I add, the pizza buffet was magnificent!

Back to the moment when something flipped in me, and the defining question:

Why was I thoroughly terrified to do something one moment, then in the very next moment found myself willingly doing that very thing?

I'll tell you the answer I've come to: it's because I heard my name.

Now, no one was shouting "Todd Henry". That's not what I mean. You see, I've come to believe that my real name isn't whatever my parents called me, my real name is whatever I choose to respond to.

I've learned that all day long, every day I have names hurled at me by my circumstances. My inner narrator hears things like "coward", or "imposter", or "incompetent", or "selfish", or "failure".

However, I've trained myself to spot those narratives as they enter my head because I've learned that more often than not, the narrative or vision that I choose to listen to will be the dominant influencer of my behavior.

So, in that moment, instead of responding to the name

"coward", putting my head down, and trying not to make eye contact with our guide, I chose to respond to the name "brave."

I chose - in that moment - to live by the narrative that we've taught our kids since a young age that we do hard things. In fact, the likely reason that Ava sped to the front of the line is because since she was young we've called her "Br-Ava" to reinforce that she is courageous and doesn't need to be timid. We've reinforced that name for her, so her natural response with her life is toward bravery.

We each stand at various precipices in our lives, and in those moments we must choose our identity. Will you be the kind of person who shrinks from the moment, or the one who is willing - even when it's uncomfortable - to do the right thing? Will you not only endure, but *embrace* discomfort for the sake of the greater good? Will you refuse to rationalize cowardly behavior as an expression of wisdom?

Will you respond to the name "brave"?

HOW DO YOU MEASURE A LIFE?

This is a question that innovation theorist Clayton Christensen asked in a fantastic book by the same title. He said that many of his contemporaries from business school had found themselves in jail because, despite their financial success, they didn't set good boundaries for their life and eventually violated common ethical or legal standards. They had not pre-established how much was enough, so when they found themselves with the opportunity to gain a little more they simply couldn't help themselves.

So, I ask you the same question: how will you measure your life? In years lived? In experiences? In the amount of money you accumulate? In how others think of you, or your reputation in your community?

The truth is, you cannot really control any of those things. One unfortunate illness or accident and your years could be cut short unexpectedly, due to no fault of your own. Despite your best intent, your health may compromise the quality of the experiences you can genuinely have. While you may chase financial success, any number of forces beyond your control can cause all of that money to slip through your fingers. And despite all the good that you may do in your community, your reputation and legacy are beyond your ability to control. It will be a story that others tell once you're gone.

So, how do you measure a life? I propose a simple answer: in the number of moments in which you overcame cowardice and acted bravely.

Those moments of bravery form the shape of your life and also its depth. Perhaps more importantly, they carve meaning into the mountainside of mundanity. When you think back on your life, the moments you will be most proud of are those in which you choose action over apathy, candor over cowardice, and intercession over feigned ignorance.

Most people will never see or even know about these

moments. They are yours alone, and they define your character, which in turn determines your destiny. And in the end, they are the foundation of your life's story.

ANTHONY AND HIS DIAGNOSIS

Anthony was a high school teacher in Brunei, on the island of Borneo. While teaching he was unexpectedly diagnosed with a brain tumor and given a year to live. Wanting to ensure that his young wife wasn't left penniless when he died, he hatched a plan to write and sell a few novels to provide a sum for her to live on after he was gone. In the next year, he worked feverishly, writing and selling four novels to publishers, successfully executing his plan. However, it turns out the doctors were wrong. There was never a tumor. His frantic writing pace was unnecessary, only brought upon by the urgency of his imminent death.

During the year of 1959-60, Anthony Burgess wrote *The Doctor Is Sick* (1960), *Inside Mr. Enderby* (1963), *The Worm and the Ring* (1961), *The Wanting Seed* (1962), and *One Hand Clapping* (1961). He would later produce his most well-known work *A Clockwork Orange*, which would be immortalized in film by Stanley Kubrick. In later years, Burgess referred to this prolific period as his "terminal year", because he was writing against the clock knowing he was about to die. Despite his false diagnosis, he lived to age seventy-six, eventually succumbing in 1993.

It's amazing what we can accomplish when we believe that

we are running out of time. The ironic thing is, we are. Every single one of us has a finite number of days on this planet, and each new day means that we are getting closer to our inevitable end. I don't say this to depress you, but rather to instill a sense of urgency about how you approach your days.

If you knew you had exactly one year left on this planet, what would you do? And, why aren't you doing it? To be fair, we have to behave responsibly and with an eye on the future, which is why I despise the advice "live each day like it's your last." However, as you consider your ideas, your dreams, your relationships, your ambitions, which of them are you deferring action on until a more convenient time? In truth, that time may never come.

I encourage you to consider the next year of your life a "terminal" year. What if you knew that on this date one year from today you would be dead? How would it change the way you approach your relationships, your work, your friendships, and the kinds of decisions that you make every day?

Would it cause you to behave more bravely?

Would it help you connect to what really matters?

Might it open your eyes to ways in which you're deferring your ambitions?

Here's a short fifteen-minute exercise that might help you gain some clarity:

1. Take out a piece of paper and at the top write the date one year from today.

2. Spend about ten minutes considering what you'd like to be different on that date. How will you have changed? Who will you have impacted? What will you have built?

3. Now, cross out anything that is outside of your sphere of influence. Don't focus on what you can't control.

4. With the remaining items, write one small action step that you can take in the next week to begin you on the journey of accomplishing it. The key is to make it small. It should almost feel easy.

5. Keep this list with you. When you take your small step, write another one down. Then, do it.

Yes, this almost sounds too easy and simplistic. However, every great accomplishment occurs through small, measured progress made with urgency and diligence.

ONE

That's the number of days you are given. Today is that day.

Tomorrow is still to be determined, yet we spend so much time worrying about things that are still in flux, that we may have no influence over. We waste mental cycles catastrophizing and allowing fear to fun rampant. We become paralyzed with inaction because we are afraid of getting it wrong, and the implications that could have on our future.

Because we are terrified of what *might* happen, we lose sight of our agency to make things happen through brave action. We lose sight of all that we've accomplished until now and the skills and platform we've developed that uniquely positions us to affect the change we desire.

You *will* get it wrong. That's a certainty. It's not a matter of if, it's a matter of when and to what degree. But being wrong is of no importance, really. Right or wrong isn't what separates brilliant achievers from the rest, it's their willingness to adjust, adapt, and bravely move forward in the face of setbacks. It's their courage to ride the waves of uncertainty rather than being overcome by them.

Don't fear wrong action, fear *inaction*. Stagnancy is the specter that should keep you awake at night more than any other.

One small step in the face of fear is enough to dispel its hold on you. Regular, measured steps in the direction of your optimistic vision is sufficient to generate unstoppable momentum. When your big breakthrough comes, it probably won't feel momentous. Rather, it will seem like the next logical step in a long chain of brave actions. Success comes in layers and is earned through consistency. Consistency breeds confidence, which breeds courage.

And consistency begins with a choice to show up and seize the moment.

So, what will you do with your *one* day? What small, brave actions will you choose?

Will you choose to be a reconciler of relationships by forgiving instead of assigning blame?

Will you choose to share your idea with your manager instead of giving in to the fear of ridicule?

Will you choose to make something - *anything* - that moves you closer to your long-deferred ambition instead of saying "someday I'll…"?

Will you choose to approach that client who seems out of reach instead of falling prey to imposter syndrome?

Each of these choices, and thousands of others in your life, are singular moments in time that establish a new vector for you. What you choose to do with them will ultimately determine whether you build a body of work you can point to with pride, or one which reflects your complacency, fear, and lack of nerve.

I cannot emphasize enough how urgent this day is for you. You must treat it like your only valuable asset, because it is.

And within that precious day is a singular moment for you to seize.

What is it, and what will you do with it?

Be brave.

You've reached the end of the book, but there are more resources to help you on your path to courageous leadership.

Visit **TheBraveHabit.com** for:

The Brave Habit workbook

The Brave Index assessment

The Brave Habit course

Videos, podcast episodes, and more

ACKNOWLEDGEMENTS

I'm grateful for the encouragement of my friends and family who patiently listened to me talk about the ideas in this book for years as I was working them out in my head. Now, here they are on paper. Your brave patience has paid off.

The first person to put courage into me to share these ideas more broadly was my friend Chris Flanagan. As an elementary school principal, he asked if he could share my thoughts on bravery vs. boldness with his team. Sadly, we lost Chris in 2023, and I can think of no one who better exemplified living a brave life. The seeds he planted will grow up into mighty oaks.

Thank you to those who allowed me to share their story in this book, and to those who modeled bravery in a way that brought these concepts to life.

To those who emailed me after hearing these ideas in a podcast episode or through reading one of my articles to tell me they were inspired by them, thank you for pushing me to write this book. I hope you find it helpful in your journey.

Thank you to my literary agent Melissa White for helping me navigate the waters.

To my family, and especially my wife Rachel, I'm grateful for the encouragement to pursue my ideas and passion. You inspire me every day and make me want to be brave.

To you, dear reader, for doing the right thing even when it may cost you. We need you to be brave. Let's do this together.

ABOUT THE AUTHOR

Todd Henry is the author of seven books (*The Accidental Creative, Die Empty, Louder Than Words, Herding Tigers, The Motivation Code, Daily Creative, The Brave Habit*) which have been translated into more than a dozen languages. With nearly 20 million downloads, his podcast has provided weekly inspiration for creative professionals since 2005. Todd speaks, trains, and consults around the world on the topics of creativity, leadership, and passion for work.

Learn more at **ToddHenry.com**.

KEYNOTES AND WORKSHOPS

Todd Henry delivers keynotes and workshops around the world on a variety of topics related to *The Brave Habit*, including:

Developing The Brave Habit
Brave Leadership
Habits Of Brave Teams

If you'd like to explore bringing Todd Henry to your organization or event to teach about these topics, or any of his books, visit **ToddHenry.com/speaking**.

Printed in the USA
CPSIA information can be obtained
at www.ICGtesting.com
JSHW080935230424
61676JS00004BB/20

9 798218 303419